The Tourist and
the Real Japan

The Tourist and the Real Japan

How to avoid pitfalls and get the most out of your trip

BOYE DE MENTE

CHARLES E. TUTTLE COMPANY
Rutland, Vermont & Tokyo, Japan

Other Books by Boye De Mente

De Mente Taxi Guide to Tokyo
Traveler's Language Guide to Japan
Bachelor's Japan
Bachelor's Hawaii
Bachelor's Mexico
Once a Fool: From Tokyo to Alaska by Amphibious Jeep
Oriental Secrets of Graceful Living
How Business is Done in Japan
Japanese Manners & Ethics in Business

Representatives

For Continental Europe:
BOXERBOOKS, INC., *Zurich*

For the British Isles:
PRENTICE-HALL INTERNATIONAL, INC., *London*

For Australasia:
BOOK WISE (AUSTRALIA) PTY. LTD.
104-108 Sussex Street, Sydney 2000

Published by the Charles E. Tuttle Company, Inc.
of Rutland, Vermont & Tokyo, Japan
with editorial offices at
Suido 1-chome, 2-6, Bunkyo-ku, Tokyo, Japan

Copyright in Japan, 1963 by Boye De Mente

Library of Congress Catalog Card No. 67-15318

International Standard Book No. 0-8048-0593-8

First printing, 1967
Tenth printing, 1982

PRINTED IN JAPAN

To the traveler who finds, as I have, that
despite the pitfalls Japan is a fascinating country.

I very gratefully acknowledge my debt to the many friends and travelers whose experiences have been recorded or referred to in this book. Several of them will no doubt return this gratitude when they find their identities unrevealed.

Contents

The Fairyland 11

The Real Japan 14

The "Ugly" Tourist 17

What Do You Really Want to Accomplish? 20

"The Japanese Way" 22

A Code of Manners 25

The Importance of "Face" 29

The Myth of Politeness 34

The "Unimportance" of Time 38

The Language Problem 41

Beware of Japan's Labyrinths! 53

Weather...for Better or Worse 57

"Packing Them In" 59

The Traveler: His Stomach and Manners 66

Prices High and Low 72

Is Bargaining Necessary? 77

Good Guides and Bad 81

On the Pratice of Tipping 87

The Toilet—A "Convenient Place" 90

The Business of Pleasure 98

Mixed Bathing for Everybody 102

Should You Stay on the Beaten Track 108

Why Visit Japan? 121

Every Traveler's Problem 130

The "Secret" of Japan's Success 135

A Capsule History 141

I *The Fairyland*

To the average person who has never been to Japan, the country is apt to be a kind of fairyland made up of colorfully dressed women, awe-inspiring shrines, picturesque "Oriental" scenery and various other sights and sounds of an exotic and fascinating nature, all presided over by a "peerless" mountain perpetually capped in snow.

This idea owes its origin to a number of factors. First, and most important, many of the sights and sounds of Japan are indeed exotic and fabulous. Second, the Japanese since the country began intercourse with the West have made a determined and largely successful effort to hide the true Japan from the foreigner, to display only a particular face, painted and masked, to the gullible outsider. Third, the travel industry, both Japanese and foreign, emphasizes the fairyland aspect of the country and avoids the slightest hint that there might be more to Japan than what is presented in its "literature" . . . whether it is good or bad. Hollywood has also contributed to the general conception that Japan is a "postcard" country.

For the most part, the Japanese sincerely believe that their country is truly a sightseer's paradise; that next to Japan most other nations fade into ignominy. They believe this because only an infinitesimal number have ever been to a Western country and are therefore able to make a comparison, and also because of an extreme and distinctive form of pride in the peculiarities, the uniqueness and the arbitrarily believed superiority of things Japanese, whether it concerns a dwarf tree or a coastline.

The foreign members of the industry featuring Japan as a travel area restrict themselves to only the most idyllic and fascinating aspects of the country's tourist attractions because it is good business.

The potential traveler is spoon-fed a diet of provocative, vision-conjuring descriptions of the pliable Geisha, of Japan festooned from one end to the other in fragile cherry blossoms, of gay festivals that go on and on, and of glimpses into a strange and—in some instances—glorious past. The traveler is told that he may have all this without worry or strain, that he will be more pampered and indulged than he is in his own home.

Many foreigners who have made a considerable effort to see and experience Japan in a little more depth than usual, have severely criticized the Japan travel industry—along with its foreign elements—when they were unable to accomplish their purpose and got very little or no encouragement from the industry. At the same time, there have been many others who responded wholeheartedly to the blandishments of travel industry publicity and actually found their tour of Japan the fulfilment of all promises. This latter group, however, is a rapidly decreasing minority. It cannot be denied that Japan is unusual, exotic, fascinating, enigmatic; and as such is one of the most interesting and worthwhile lands a foreigner could visit. At the same time, it is not the complete paradise for tourists that the industry would have us believe.

II *The Real Japan*

For nearly every feature of Japan that serves to make the country attractive as a tourist area, there is an opposing feature that often detracts from this attractiveness . . . and cannot be entirely covered up or disguised by the travel industry. After weighing these plus and minus factors, whether or not a visit to the real Japan is worth the time, trouble and money, depends both upon the efforts of the travel industry and the taste and expectations of the individual traveler—both of which tend to be capricious or ignorant . . . the industry of what it should be doing and how it should be doing it, and the traveler of what he wants and expects.

Behind the mask that Japan presents to the outside world there is much to attract and please the foreign visitor. There is also much that is ugly and inhumane. Most of what Japan presents to outsiders as being the genius and pride of the Japanese is actually the result of stark necessity and compromise forced onto the people over many centuries. The foreign visitor who gushes over the wonderfully "polite" manners of the people would be shocked and repelled if he knew the insidiously brutal social sanctions brought to bear upon the Japanese to condition them to behave in this manner. The foreigner would be even more shocked at the suggestion that since he finds traditional Japanese behavior so attractive he should try conducting himself in the same manner.

The real Japan is not made up of only gorgeous temples, grand palaces, imposing castles, superbly "simple" gardens, exotically costumed girls and Kabuki actors. These carefully preserved vestiges of an inglorious history of suffering and servitude—under a regime which perverted this suffering and servitude into the highest virtues—are only a small part of Japan.

The real Japan is the countless hours—sometimes decades—of painstaking labor that went into making a Japanese garden look like the essence of simplicity; the numbing cold that pervades the aesthetically pleasing homes of the Japanese in winter; the lifetime of eating fish, soy bean gruel, rice and pickles; students lining up to sell their blood so they can buy books; farm men and women working year after year bent over in the fields until finally they can no longer straighten up and have to live out the rest of their lives as horrible caricatures of human beings; the millions of small people who spend their lives in tiny cubby holes, shops and factories for just enough to keep alive; the poverty, the ignorance and the pride that have shaped many of the peculiar customs and habits of the Japanese . . . this is the real Japan.

But the traveler sees very little of this. He stays on a well-beaten path that takes him to modern buildings, well-stocked stores in the larger cities, plush hotels, the best bars, cabarets and night-clubs. He is systematically paraded past those relics of Old Japan that are calculated to impress the foreigner, but the closest he gets to seeing the country and people is as he glimpses them in passing.

It is too much to expect that a traveler who is going to be in Japan for only a few days, or a few weeks at most, can visit more than a few places, meet more than a few people, or experience more than a few facets of Japan. It also cannot be expected that the traveler will have complete control over what he will see and do. This is generally all arranged for him beforehand by people who may or may not know what they are doing.

There are, however, a number of steps that can be taken to improve one's chances of really enjoying a trip to Japan and getting something worthwhile out of it. The first problem the traveler has to face is himself.

III *The "Ugly" Tourist*

Most American travelers to the Orient are "ugly" at some time or other during their journey because they say and do things without thinking. They have traveled many thousands of miles and spent a considerable amount of money to see and experience things that cannot be seen or experienced in any other part of the world. Yet they often complain bitterly if they have to give up any of the conveniences of the West in order to see a bit of the East.

In his more rational moments, the average traveler realizes full well that a cook in a small restaurant in Takamatsu on Shikoku island may never have heard of an egg "over easy", may not be able to brown toast like the traveler gets at home in New York or San Francisco. But it is amazing how many travelers forget what they know when they are confronted with something that is different from what they are used to.

In Nikko I have heard a party of several women scathingly criticize the management of one of the better hotels there because part of their dinner was served to them cold. In Atami I have heard a bus load of tourists who had just come over the mountain from Hakone complain of the irresponsibility of the Japan Travel Bureau in allowing them to come over such a narrow and precarious road. I have also heard tourists complain loud and long that most of the Japanese with whom they came into contact couldn't speak enough English, that shops catering to foreign travelers charged higher prices than other places, that public transportation was too crowded, that it was impossible for them to step outside of their hotel without a guide, and so on.

Much of this complaining is not very serious. Americans, particularly, seem to get into the habit of complaining and it becomes something of a pastime with them, whether there is cause or not. What these people ignore or don't know is that they are making a spectacle of themselves and insulting their hosts—even when there are, from their viewpoint, legitimate reasons for complaining.

The Japanese are inordinately indulgent of the whims and idiosyncrasies of foreigners and go to extreme lengths to please them most of the time. But despite their almost fawning acceptance of criticism, they cannot help but feel that this type of behavior is insulting and that people who behave in this way are their cultural inferiors. In any event, travelers can rest assured that the faults and sore points they so vociferously point out have been pointed out before, and they are not about to revolutionize the travel industry in Japan by making a few clerks or small hotel proprietors lose face.

Fortunately, from this viewpoint, tourists traveling through Japan are generally confined to narrow, well-defined routes and the people they meet very quickly become calloused to their strange ways and act as a buffer between them and the people at large. Foreigners who are shocked at the idea of Japanese men urinating in the streets would probably be surprised to learn that some of the things they do while in Japan are considered barbaric and beneath any self-respecting Japanese.

Most Americans who travel to Japan naturally do not speak the language and know little or nothing about the way the Japanese live and think.   It is therefore understandable that they will often commit errors of etiquette and sometimes bluntly insult the Japanese.   As a matter of fact, the Japanese expect them to make mistakes and would no doubt be disappointed if they didn't.   But many Americans become especially thinskinned when they get outside the U.S. and it doesn't take much to bring out the "Hyde" in them.   Others become keyed up because of the pace and excitement of their travels and are likely to flare up at the slightest provocation.

There is also the important consideration that because most travelers to Japan really don't have a good idea of what they can or should get out of their trip, they are prone to be more critical and much more apt to be disappointed if things fall short of what amounts to a hazy but high ideal.

IV *What Do You Really Want to Accomplish?*

Many travelers, after doggedly taking in a long list of shrines, temples, monuments and scenic spots in Japan, have confessed just before they were to leave the country that they were not at all satisfied and felt they had not even been close to coming into intimate contact with the Japanese. On some of these occasions, I have been able to take the people concerned to a few places in Tokyo, explain something of the present-day culture and psychology of the Japanese to them, pointing out specific examples as we went along, and have the travelers assure me that this last few hours had made their trip worthwhile.

This very common occurrence points up two failings: the inability of the local Japanese travel industry to understand and fulfill the desires of all foreign visitors, and second, the failure of the traveler himself to seriously consider—beforehand—what he wants from his trip.

Since the failings of the Japanese travel industry are traditional as well as inherent—and therefore impervious to all but the most gradual change—my advice in this book will be aimed at helping the traveler help himself. Before making some general as well as some specific suggestions as to what the traveler should do to get the most out of his trip, it is necessary to first consider the obstacles involved in traveling in Japan and the extent to which they restrict the traveler's prerogative.

V "The Japanese Way"

Despite a Western veneer that rests lightly on the surface of many Japanese, especially those the average traveler meets, as a whole the people of Japan are not modern or cosmopolitan in the present-day Western sense of these terms. The physical and intellectual isolation of the country combined with the circumstances that allow only a few Japanese to travel abroad, makes them as provincial and as ignorantly proud as the most backward hill-tribe in Kentucky.

Knowing nothing about the outside world until recently, and very little still yet, the Japanese long ago developed a society based on a rigidly stereotyped form of behavior and prescribed attitudes that makes them unique in the world. This web of thought and manners which began to flower more than a thousand years ago, has been inherited and strengthened by each succeeding generation, and is now generally referred to as "the Japanese Way".

It is practically impossible to stay in Japan for more than a few hours without having this meaningful phrase thrown up at you, since it is used to acknowledge praise for things Japanese one moment and as an excuse for unpleasant or shocking things the next. While the traveler in Japan can get along without any knowledge of "the Japanese Way," his trip will have a great deal more meaning if he knows something about it.

The fact that most foreign visitors to Japan over the years knew nothing about the country resulted in their looking upon the Japanese, superficially at least, as Alice-in-Wonderland creatures who were quaint and charming and not to be taken seriously. However, the traveler who looks upon the "politeness" and other unusual customs of the Japanese and thinks of them as "quaint" might well reflect upon the fact that most of the characteristics and habits of the Japanese that Westerners praise so highly are the result of centuries of oppression and rigid conditioning that most people would not wish upon an animal.

The traveler should therefore exercise enlightened judgment not only in what he praises but also in what he may be tempted to condemn unreasonably. There very often is no excuse for the failure of the Japanese to change or improve their methods or manners when internationally recognized modes of thought and manner dictate such changes, but there is a compelling reason for their being the way they are in the first place.

Distinctive characteristics of the Japanese with which the traveler will come into contact—no matter how much he is insulated from the public-at-large—include the "myth" of politeness, the importance of "face", the unimportance of time, the propensity of the Japanese to become flustered, to laugh when they are embarrassed or don't understand what is going on or being said, the deeply ingrained habit of refusing to admit lack of knowledge, and others.

VI   *A Code of Manners*

It is difficult for the Western mind to grasp just how important manners are to the Japanese in all facets of life. Westerners are generally conditioned to conduct their lives according to certain abstract principles, with manners playing only a minor role. In Japan, the pendulum swung the other way and a society was forged in which the ultimate virtue was a prescribed conduct. Morality as it is known in the West was incidental.

Since around the 6th Century A.D., or nearly fourteen hundred years ago, the Japanese have been more concerned with form than with sincerity or accomplishment. The people were required to walk a certain way, to sit a certain way, to open doors a certain way, to sleep with their heads pointing in a certain way and with their legs arranged in a certain way. The style and manner of their dress was prescribed by law. Their manner of eating was severely prescribed, they could enter a house only a certain way, greet each other only a certain way. Even physical movements necessary to perform many types of work were definitely established and no deviation was allowed.

So rigid and so severe were these prescribed manners that they long ago became a part of the Japanese character—permeating and shaping every part of their lives. "The Japanese Way" which most travelers learn about shortly after their arrival in Japan is a result of this meticulous conditioning.

Japan's history is full of the most amazing, shocking incidents of what happened to people who behaved in an "other than expected manner"—i.e. other than the Japanese way. One of the most quoted of these incidents involved a farmer named Sogo who went over the head of his local lord in 1760 to complain of starvation taxes to Japan's military dictator. For having broken a rule of etiquette, Sogo was forced to watch his three small sons beheaded. Then he and his wife were crucified—although his complaint proved justified and the local lord was removed from office.

This, of course, involved extraordinary circumstances, but Japanese society was explicitly demanding in all matters, including the most trivial. It was considered an extreme insult, for example, to touch a superior person or sit in any but a prescribed way while in his presence, and resulted in swift, harsh punishment for anyone foolish enough to forget "proper" manners. Japan's most famous true drama, the story of forty-seven samurai who killed themselves after avenging their master's death, happened because a man was given faulty instructions in matters of etiquette.

Japanese society was therefore utterly cruel in

that a man's morals were *visible for all to see.* For many centuries, a breach of etiquette was just as much a crime as murder or robbery is in the West. And the broken rule of conduct that made the death penalty inevitable did not have to be very important from our point of view.

Just a few decades ago it was legal for a member of the *Samurai* class (privileged military) to immediately kill anyone from a lower class who failed to show him proper respect; and the *Samurai* were among the most arrogant and status-conscious men that have ever lived.

Perhaps worse than this was the fact that whenever a Japanese failed to live up to his obligations or was remiss in his manners toward anyone, he lost his place in life. This, still today, is an important consideration in the lives of the Japanese.

There are innumerable daily examples of Japan's code of manners in action. In schools and homes, effort is still being made to instill into the students' minds the belief that form and manner are more important than ideas or accomplishments; with the result that the Japanese are literally trained to perform rather than educated, a disadvantage that weighs on them heavily when they are dealing with foreigners.

Merely because the Japanese businessman considers it bad manners to bring up problems or unexpected circumstances soon after they occur, he will very often allow a situation to develop that causes him or an importer to lose thousands of dollars. A recent example: An importer placed an order for several thousand dollars worth of ceramics and was promised delivery on a certain date. As the date began to draw near, the supplier started asking for extensions. The delivery date came and went and the importer not only lost sales but reputation as well. He then discovered that the supplier was selling the merchandise that had been made for him to a second buyer who had come in and offered the maker a better deal. The supplier felt that "it would have caused an awkward situation" to let the first buyer know what was going on.

The visitor who is in Japan for only a few days may not run afoul of the negative side of this characteristic—if his trip is planned in detail and he doesn't upset his schedule in any way. On the contrary, the visitor is generally overwhelmed by what, on the surface, amounts to a truly remarkable display of controlled behavior—and in effect is still the essence of Japanese society, in which the "Golden Rule" has been perfect hierarchal harmony at any human cost.

VII *The Importance of "Face"*

Americans are familiar with the idea of "losing face" as it applies to the Japanese. The idea and the words have been bandied about for a number of years, but few appreciate the significance of the terms or how important the idea of face is to everyday business and social life in Japan. To lose face means much more to a Japanese than what being embarrassed or insulted means to Americans, except in the very strongest sense of the words.

Perhaps one of the best ways to illustrate the very great sensitivity of the Japanese and their susceptibility to insults would be to liken it to the glorified Hollywood version of the cowboy villain who is ready to fight to the death at the slightest offense.

Although such great sensitivity to all outside influences is a tremendous handicap for the Japanese, it is not something that they can take off like a coat. It is a part of their national character, and comes under what is referred to as *giri* to one's name.

All Japanese must have *giri* to their name, and it is especially important for people who have professional status of any kind or degree. Maintaining their face or reputation as a professional person, however, does not mean that they have to be skilled in their line of work or conduct themselves ethically. It means, instead, that they cannot in *giri* to their name admit ignorance or inability! If a foreigner asks a Japanese manufacturer whether or not he can make a certain item, the manufacturer would lose face if he said he could not. If the Japanese businessman is on the verge of bankruptcy he cannot let anyone know about it because of *giri* to his name. Japanese firms and organizations cannot admit that they do not have anyone on their staff capable of writing English, so they continue to hash the language up like it was so much putty. Each year, a number of Japanese kill themselves because they failed to keep *giri* to their name.

One of the most common ways the Japanese have of avoiding the loss of face is to ignore any situation that might prove embarrassing. When they do this in relatively unimportant social contexts—as when a host refuses to acknowledge the presence of a guest until he is ready to receive him formally—it is of no particular consequence. When it takes place in business activity—as it does daily—the results are often far reaching.

The Japanese believe it is the height of rudeness and vulgarity to come out in the open and state opinions or unpleasant truths frankly. Whereas Americans generally are in the habit of "laying all their cards on the table." The Japanese have been conditioned to speak vaguely and when necessary resort to deception rather than make a frank statement that might give offense. This basic difference in attitudes and manners puts both Japanese and Americans

one extreme or the other. They either complain and criticize too much or are overly effusive in their praise. Over the years, the latter type has probably done Japan more harm than could be imagined. Feeling inferior in many respects, the Japanese have made a cult of seeking the approval and praise of foreigners for any idea or thing native to Japan. And foreigners, sensing this need, have lavished so much indiscriminate praise on Japan for so long that the Japanese live in a kind of dream world in which they are able to keep themselves more or less convinced that in the more important aspects of life they are above all other people.

Again, there is much in Japan to praise. Many of their habits, and their reverence for natural beauty as expressed in the term *shibui*, are worthy of universal emulation. But the stop-over foreigner who automatically bubbles over with laudation for every strange thing he sees in Japan is generally not exercising any judgment. He is un-thinkingly equating strangeness with merit and quality . . . and doing no one a favor.

VIII   *The Myth of Politeness*

The first-time visitor to Japan is always struck by the wonderful "politeness" of the people. No other Japanese trait or accomplishment has come in for so much praise. But most of it is not really politeness as Westerners understand and use the word. It does not stem primarily from feelings of kindness, regard or respect for others—although most Japanese are, of course, perfectly capable of being polite in the fullest sense of the word. What the foreigner sees, and is impressed by, is a strictly mechanical form which is learned by rote from earliest babyhood and has nothing or very little to do with the personal feelings or inclinations of the people concerned.

Many Americans, especially tourists, heap praise upon the Japanese for this apparent politeness. And it has now got to the point where many Japanese believe that they deserve this praise. Most foreign visitors to Japan base their judgment of Japanese politeness upon such things as the pretty, doll-like elevator and escalator girls who work in department stores. These girls, picked for looks and dressed in cute uni-

34

forms, stand and bow and repeat the same lines all day long in self-effacing, heart-rending voices that remind one of the chirping of baby birds that have fallen out of their nests.

Visiting foreigners also claim that because of the politeness of the Japanese, service in Japanese stores is superior to that found in American stores. But this doesn't hold up under ordinary circumstances. When a group of tourists or businessmen visit a store, usually accompanied by guides and interpreters, they get quick—and what amounts to servile—service primarily because they are an unusual attraction and the center of attention. Long-time residents of Japan who have shopped in Japanese department stores for years testify that it is almost always necessary to chase down a clerk.

It is not customary for clerks in stores to come up to a prospective customer and ask if they can help him. They ordinarily say and do nothing until called and in case the customer is a foreigner they will often do their best to ignore him, apparently in the hope that he will go away and prevent embarrassment—as a result of language difficulties or their natural uneasiness when in the presence of a foreigner.

This characteristic of ignoring callers—which to the Western way of thinking is not only bad for business but impolite—is not reserved for potential customers in department stores. I have often gone into business offices in which there were anywhere from three to a hundred people and had to go to extreme lengths to get someone to acknowledge my presence. This is a very common occurrence and on several occasions I have gone into offices with the idea of just standing there, in the middle of everything, until someone asked me what I wanted. I invariably broke down first—out of embarrassment on my part—and said the first word.

At first, I thought this peculiar reaction was brought on by the fact that I was a foreigner. Since a Japanese usually never expects a foreigner to be able to speak his language, I was prepared to believe that they hesitated to say anything because no one could speak English, or were simply bashful. I soon noticed, however, that Japanese visitors got the same treatment.

Further observations taught me how to shorten the period of waiting—at least in a business office—but direct action on my part was still required. This consisted of catching the eye of anyone in the office who glanced up at me and bowing very rapidly before he or she could turn away. The most effective bow to use in this situation is a short jerky bow, something like ducking your head the way a chicken does. This action triggers an automatic reflex and the other party bows back, thus acknowledging that he sees you and preparing the way for the next step.

Government employees and members of large firms are the worst offenders in this category. Foreigners dealing with Japanese, especially those visiting Japan for the first time, are advised to keep in mind the fact that the Japanese are excessively "courteous" and seemingly easy to prevail upon because it is their way of defending themselves and accomplishing their own ends, not because they are so fond of the foreign visitor that they just cannot refuse him anything.

In this respect, travelers are lucky. The primary purpose of most of the Japanese they meet in hotels, restaurants, shops, etc., is to cater to their guests . . . and at this the Japanese have few rivals. Personal service, when there is no foreign element involved to befuddle the persons concerned, has been close to a fine art in Japan for nearly two thousand years. The highly formalized and servile attitudes characterizing Japanese manners toward each other and outsiders alike, in fact, makes the foreigner feel like some kind of a minor god.

IX *The "Unimportance" of Time*

Another national habit of the Japanese which au-
dibly grates on the nerves of hurried—and often har-
ried—visitors is their apparent indifference to time.
The Japanese have not yet been conditioned to consider that time is money, that the faster one moves
or works the more he can get done. They get no
satisfaction out of doing things quickly and do not
fully appreciate the reasons why anyone else would
want to; even, it seems, when there are perfectly valid reasons for urgency. There are individual
cases in which they speed things up and on occasion
they may rush about frantically, but generally speaking, they have an aversion to hurried actions of any
kind.

The "Japanese way" opposes the idea of speed.
Comparing the nature of the Japanese with that of
the turtle is a rather strained analogy but they have
been conditioned for milleniums to do things only
after obtuse deliberations and to perform all actions
in a slow, prescribed manner. This characteristic is
magnified considerably in the eyes of the busy visitor

who not only approves wholeheartedly of reasonable haste but is almost always on a tight schedule and is particularly sensitive to signs of unreasonable—and what appears to him uncooperative—slowness.

In everyday business intercourse between Japanese and foreigners this trait can be very frustrating, and at times seriously impede the operation of business. Saul Sutton, of I. S. Sutton & Sons, a major New York importing firm, pointed out (during his thirty-fourth business trip to Japan in twelve years) that most Japanese seem incapable of appreciating how important time is to a foreign businessman, especially one that has traveled ten thousand miles to see them. He said that exporters and manufacturers regularly made appointments with him and then showed up hours late or not at all and then offered no reason.

Foreigners living and working in Japan are continuously plagued by this situation in daily matters. Laundry, film in the shop for developing, a suit at the tailors, a job around the house or almost anything involving time is rarely done when promised or expected. This propensity to move slowly and be late is not something reserved for foreigners. The Japanese are even more indifferent to time when other Japanese are concerned. They demonstrate very little if any sympathy for each other in many cases but the custom is particularly noticeable in business matters or matters of convenience.

For example, a company owes a bill and since most bills in Japan have to be collected in person, someone is sent to pick up the money. The bill collector may travel for an hour or more to reach the company concerned only to be told that the payment isn't ready. A question as to when it will be ready very often draws an indefinite answer and the collector will continue meekly visiting the company until they decide to pay. This sometimes goes on for weeks and generally it will happen at least once whether it is money or some other matter.

This waste of time and effort could be avoided but doing so would break several codes and manners that shackle the Japanese to this type of behavior. These manners include a very strong reluctance to handle or talk about money. To hand a person money that is not in an envelope or wrapped up in paper is grossly impolite and may be taken as a strong insult. There is also a strong tendency to delay payment of bills as long as possible even when the money is available.

The traveler who has only a limited time in Japan—and generally wants to make the most of it—can run into serious trouble if he waits until the last minute to make arrangements, even those that are simple and routine. I have watched and heard hundreds of visitors in travel offices reduce themselves to nervous wrecks trying to set up a two-hour trip to Nikko or some similar place.

Best way to avoid this problem if you must make arrangements after arriving in Japan is to engage one of the smaller, independent—and therefore considerably more efficient—local agencies to handle all details for you.

X *The Language Problem*

A number of years ago, I worked for a short period in the Overseas Travel Section of the Japan Travel Bureau. As the only foreigner in the department, I stood out conspicuously from my co-workers; often, it turned out, much to my embarrassment. For whenever there was any difficulty involving a traveler from abroad I was frequently pulled into it.

The foreign visitor, spying what he felt would be a kindred spirit, would gradually gravitate my way and the Japanese that he had first approached, sensing this, encouraged the movement until finally there would be no choice but to join the conversation. Then it was left up to me.

Most of the complaints concerned fouled up schedules, reservations, or simple misunderstandings stemming from the language problem. A majority of the Japanese who are employed in the tourist trade and supposedly speak and understand English, actually have a very poor command of the language. Except in rare cases, however, they will not take this into consideration when dealing with a foreigner but will try to take care of him without being able to fully understand what he says or wants. This, of course, results in misunderstandings.

Seasoned travelers have worked out various systems to avoid this important problem. Some of them write out in simple English all the basic information concerning their travel plans and go through it step by step with the travel clerk, making sure that every point is thoroughly understood before passing on to the next one.

Many travelers get themselves into trouble by automatically assuming that everyone they come into contact with in a travel bureau, hotel or shop catering to tourists speaks and understands fluent English. Generally they do not. Up until recently, foreign language instruction in Japan was even less effective than what it is in the United States—if that is possible. Students learned, after many laborious years, to read English with some facility but they were unable to advance beyond this because there was no way they could learn speaking and hearing.

Most of the English language instructors in Japan cannot speak or understand spoken English and they naturally cannot teach students what they themselves don't know. The average adult Japanese has "studied" English for several years but cannot manage to do more than parrot a few stock phrases and understand even less.

While it is pathetic that so many people have spent so much time learning so little, the language situation in Japan is improving rapidly, and has its humorous aspects if you have the time and inclination to appreciate them.

Since the days of Perry most of Japan's proud *sensei* (professors) have refused to let their own inabilities bother them. When they were called upon to teach English the fact that they could neither pronounce it properly nor understand it when it was spoken was nothing to be concerned about. They taught it—and still teach it—as if it were Japanese. That is, they pronounce it in Japanese. "Good morning" becomes "gu-do mo-ni-n-gu"; "thank you very much" becomes "sa-n-kyu beri muchi"; etc.

Many Japanese, who understand only snatches of English conversation spoken at the normal speed, can understand fairly well if you speak very slowly and break the words up into Japanese syllables, e.g. truck (to-ra-ku); apple pie (a-pu-ru-pai); blue bird (bu-ru ba-do). This idea that English can be pronounced in Japanese is so deeply embedded that I have had students tell me that my pronounciation was not correct and that I should be more careful.

Japan is notorious for its signs, billboards, advertising, etc. in what purports to be English, but varies from a hodge-podge of meaningless words to such "kechi" phrases as "Women Fitted in the Upper Story" on a brassiere shop marquee; "Guaranteed Pure Gold Fish" on a goldfish peddler's cart; and "Let Us Prevent Noise By Ourselves", a big traffic sign which graced Roppongi intersection in Tokyo for several years.

The English that students are required to study by their teachers is truly remarkable and of all the inane things the Japanese do in their pride and ignorance, this stands high on the list. Innumerable times students have come to me and asked for help in translating an ordinary assignment. The selections they had been given were so esoteric, so 'stream of consciousness' vague, not one in a hundred native-born English speakers could have explained them in his own tongue!

Some of the simpler examples would shock the Western student if he should be called upon to render them into some foreign tongue, e.g.:

The march of mankind is directed neither by his will, nor by his superstitions, but by the effect of his great and, as it were, accidental discoveries on his average nature. The discovery and exploitation of fire, of metals and gunpowder, of coal, steam, electricity, of flying machines, acting on human life, under all the agreeable camouflages of religions, principles, politics and ideas. The comparisons with the effect of these discoveries and their unconscious influence on human life, the affect of political ideas is seen to be inconsiderable. *

This situation is further complicated by a schizophrenic pride that generally prevents the Japanese, once they attain professional status, from either admitting that their English may be less than fluent or seeking help from someone who does know the language to advise them in proofreading publications, pamphlets, signs, etc., that are supposed to be in English. For a people who are so concerned with "face" it is difficult to understand why they continue to turn out,

---

* Anthony Scarangello, *A Fulbright Teacher in Japan*, The Hokuseido Press, Tokyo, 1957, p. 123.

in horribly mutilated English, millions of pieces of promotional literature and catalogs of all kinds that are distributed throughout the world to businessmen and others.

The answer to this paradox seems to be that so long as no one personally points out the errors to the people responsible, it is possible for them to pretend that there are no errors and no "face" is lost. And, it is considered extremely impolite for anyone to point out such mistakes, so even if there is someone in the firm or organization putting out the literature who knows better, he would not dare speak up. Many times I have seriously embarrassed various Japanese by pointing out flagrant and harmful errors in everything from menus to "White Papers" issued by Japan's Finance Ministry.

In visiting hundreds of Japanese firms, shops and other business offices in Japan, I have found that about one in twenty has someone on the staff that can speak and write English fairly well. The others usually have one or two employees who speak a sort of pidgin English and with the aid of a dictionary, laboriously turn out letters in what passes—to them —as English. Such firms never completely understand all the things the foreign visitor says or writes to them and they are almost always working in some degree of darkness. Even when information or instructions are given to a Japanese company in Japanese the possibility of a misunderstanding or failure to "get through" is enormous.

Because of both the inherent vagueness of the Japanese language and the way society and experience forces the people to use it, even well-educated Japanese have difficulty understanding each other. A few years ago it was estimated by a Tokyo University professor, whose specialty was communications, that on the first time around the Japanese are able to fully understand only about eighty-five percent of what they say to each other. Quite often there is simply no understanding at all. It is the rule that Japanese have to repeat themselves over and over again to get even simple concepts across. The language is so vague that in the most ordinary conversations people frequently have to stop and trace one or more Chinese ideographs—usually with their fingers on any surface handy or in the air—in order to communicate an idea. If the ideograph happens to be an unusual one, and there are thousands of unusual ones, or a person has forgotten it or never learned it, he may never fully understand.

Japanese was a relatively adequate language as long as the Japanese dealt only with themselves and were able and content to maintain their highly stylized, artificial society. But neither of these conditions have existed for some time now although the awkward tongue and centuries of machine-like conditioning still shackle the Japanese to their heritage. To one who is native-born and educated, its stamp is inevitable, and no matter how long they may live abroad or to what degree they may associate with foreigners, they never escape its baleful influence.

The language actually can be spoken much more directly and therefore much more effectively than it is, but to the Japanese this would be one of the worst breaches of etiquette possible. Foreigners who have a good command of Japanese are able to communicate ideas more quickly and more clearly than the Japanese, since they are not forced by habit or Japanese propriety to speak in circumlocutions. In doing so, however, they run the risk of seriously offending whomever they are talking to so it is necessary to exercise caution.

A smattering of Japanese is easy to learn and will prevent many of the situations which cause problems for the foreigner in Japan. These usually are concerned with simple desires like food, lodging, time, direction, etc., and require only a small vocabulary and little or no knowledge of grammar. A great many of the more common problems of communication occur in the first place because the foreigner assumes that any Japanese he encounters understands English.

I have watched visiting travelers and businessmen approach Japanese clerks, sales personnel, policemen and others with a question, sometimes simple and sometimes complicated, as if it was the most natural thing for them to understand English—and then be unbecomingly indignant when it turned out that they didn't.

Contrary to most people who speak a bit of some foreign tongue, the Japanese speak a great deal more than they can understand. This also misleads foreigners into believing that everything they say is understood and they go on and on and then are sorely disappointed when the Japanese concerned fails to react as expected. It is not unusual for a Japanese student or waiter to come up to a foreigner and say, in very good English, "May I help you", and then not be able to say or understand anything else.

In most cases, it is impossible to immediately tell

whether or not the Japanese concerned understands. He will say "yes" regardless of whether he did or not since it would be shameful to admit that he didn't. Besides which he is so anxious to please that he will agree to just about anything you say. About the only solution to this problem is to engage him in a bit of preliminary conversation to see how much he understands. If the topic is important and his understanding seems doubtful, the best thing to do is ask him to repeat what you said. If you write it out he may be able to read it well enough as far as pronounciation goes but there is still a possibility that he will not understand the meaning; so care must be taken.

It also seems to be customary for foreigners to believe that raising their voices and getting angry will help them communicate with a Japanese whose understanding of English is limited. They find, however, that this does not help achieve the desired result. It serves not only to further befuddle the Japanese, but in shaming him, makes him into an enemy who will never forget or forgive and one day, in some way, will take his revenge.

Foreigners who receive letters from Japanese written in adequate English are also cautioned to remember that there is an excellent chance an answering letter would not be thoroughly understood. This is not always because of inability on the part of the Japanese, however. I have examined more than a thousand letters from foreign firms to Japanese companies and found some completely incomprehensible. Many others were so general or so cryptic that much of the meaning was obscured.

More attention to a simple presentation of the

facts and less concern with impressing someone with "business" style and vocabulary would get the writers much better results.

Few foreigners visiting in Japan have not had the experience of asking a question of a Japanese—who speaks and understands some English—and getting nothing but a vacant look or a giggle in return. Even when the Japanese concerned has had a considerable amount of association with foreigners and has been asked direct questions hundreds of times, the reaction is usually the same. And unfortunately, the foreigner who does not know what lies behind this reaction immediately takes it for stupidity.

Generally, it is not stupidity but a circumstance that stems from the Japanese language, Japanese etiquette and the training Japanese receive in school. The language, first of all, is something like a mass of thin cobwebs that seem to keep the mind of the Japanese in a state of perpetual haziness that can only be penetrated by repeated efforts to make a little hole in it. Japanese etiquette, embedded into the people so deeply that it is a part of their nature, demands that directness and abrupt actions be severely avoided. When a foreigner asks an abrupt question of a Japanese who is not thoroughly accustomed to it, the Japanese is genuinely flustered and incapable of giving an answer until he collects his wits. The main reason for the blank look, however, lies in the method of instruction used in Japanese schools.

There was traditionally a complete lack of student participation in the education process. "The teacher's every word is accepted at face value; he is the expert.

The students scribble notes assiduously without questioning the meaning or substance. It is no exaggeration for me to relate that on many occasions I have asked university students questions only to find them stricken with a sort of apoplexy; speechless, their lips moved but they uttered no sound."*

Just as the average Japanese has a very difficult time responding to blunt questions, he also has a hard time expressing his feelings either verbally or otherwise with anywhere near the amount of enthusiasm expected by Americans. This characteristic is another vestige of feudal Japan when the people were required to guard their emotions on the pain of death.

This repression of emotions, in addition to being used in feudal Japan to conceal one's purpose from an enemy, was even more important as a device to enforce rigid class distinctions. Unquestioning obedience was exacted from inferiors. No questions were to be asked; no curiosity, pain, surprise, or displeasure could be displayed in the presence of a superior. Any such expression was regarded as a grave discourtesy and infringements of this code were severely punished.

Little wonder that the Japanese, after centuries of such repression, are still inclined to go about with a wooden expression and to show little emotion in ordinary as well as the most extraordinary circumstances.

There is another peculiar characteristic of the Japanese—which often has humorous overtones—that

---

* Scarangello, *A Fulbright Teacher in Japan,* p. 129

is something of a parallel problem when it happens that the foreigner speaks Japanese. There is a deep-seated belief among the Japanese that foreigners, especially Americans, cannot learn to speak Japanese. The reason for this belief is that the Japanese think their language—as well as many other aspects of Japan—is so constituted as to be impossible for anyone except a Japanese to grasp and appreciate. They are, therefore, continuously amazed to discover that a foreigner can speak their language well, and it very often happens that a foreigner will say something to a Japanese in fluent Japanese and fail to be understood.

An American lawyer who conducts cases in Japanese once walked up to a policeman in downtown Tokyo and asked him, in Japanese, if he knew the whereabouts of an address in the area. The policeman looked uncomfortable for several seconds and then finally blurted out: "I no speak English." This peeved the lawyer and he proceeded to lecture the unfortunate cop in such a loud voice that a crowd gathered.

The lawyer could probably have saved himself a lot of bother and the police officer a lot of embarrassment if he had remembered to preface his question with one of the several conversational openers which the Japanese customarily use to let the person know that you are going to speak Japanese and that he should get set to "receive" in his own language.

If one knows how to bow properly, it is possible to bow and get across the same message; but this takes more skill and experience than what might be expected, so it is safer to speak. The most effective method is to combine a bow with one of the commonly used polite prefaces. On occasion, however, this doesn't work either so there is no choice but to repeat yourself.

The traveler can, of course, get by without knowing any Japanese. But in almost every case, there will be literally hundreds of occasions when knowing just a little would make the visitor's stay in Japan a little less demanding and a great deal more interesting.

From my own experience in traveling in Japan with foreign visitors, the foreigner who doesn't know a word of Japanese must feel like someone who has washed his hands with rubber gloves on. For a man, at least, sitting next to a lovely girl at a Geisha party and not being able to say a word to her is particularly frustrating—and the lengths to which many dignified gentlemen will go in their efforts to communicate with the enigmatic Geisha ranges from hilarious to pitiful.

My advice is learn twenty-five or thirty—or more if you can—basic sentences and you will get twice as much out of your trip. A shirt-pocket size completely phoneticized Traveler's Language Guide to Japan is available at magazine and book stands in Japan for ¥150 or from many leading American bookstores for fifty cents. You should be able to master its contents in about two hours. If you can't spend that much time on study, you can carry it with you and use it as "cue cards." Other language aids of varying quality are incorporated in many of the locally available tourist publications.

XI *Beware of Japan's Labyrinths!*

Visitors to Japan are invariably surprised to learn that most streets are not named and that addresses of shops, buildings and houses have absolutely no relationship with whatever street they may be on or near! Visitors are not long in learning, however, that because of this situation it is extremely difficult even for a Japanese born and raised in the area concerned to go directly from one place to another unless he has been there before and memorized the way!

In fact, it is impossible to pinpoint any place in Japan by the address alone, as anywhere from five to fifty or more different buildings may have exactly the same address and be spread out over an area of several odd-shaped "blocks"! Furthermore, most streets, especially in Tokyo, twist and turn and disappear in dead-ends in a way that would put Minos' famous labyrinth to shame. People who have lived for fifty years in a neighborhood generally do not know the location of more than a few of the houses that have the same address as theirs, and cannot give directions to any place more than a hundred yards from where they live.

Nine times out of ten, people who live or work in a business or shopping district cannot tell you the address of the building next door to theirs. In addition to the fact that there are no street addresses and no systematic pattern of streets in most of Japan's cities, there is also no consistent, easily followed system of posting addresses that buildings do have—in any language.

Since this maze presents a tremendous obstacle to the Japanese themselves, you can imagine how much more difficult it is for a non-Japanese speaking or reading foreigner to make his way about Japan's cities without the aid of a guide. As it is now, a few travelers do venture out on their own from the downtown hotels, but unless they keep their hotel in sight or are extremely careful about how many turns they make and how far they go, they invariably get lost and are forced to wander around hoping they will run into something interesting by sheer coincidence, or have to hail a cab and get across the name of their hotel to him.

There are, of course, a number of locally published travel guides, several of which feature a certain amount of guide instructions in both Japanese and English incorporated into advertisements or on maps. Most of them, however, are oriented from the viewpoint of the foreign traveler and are therefore absolutely worthless because the foreigner is not familiar with the streets, buildings and other reference points by which he is supposed to guide himself. In the remaining cases, their value is generally limited because the information they provide is insufficient to pinpoint the place concerned.

A story recently appeared in a Tokyo newspaper that the city fathers were considering giving "nicknames" to the city's streets for the benefit of tourists. The idea of nicknaming streets just for tourists is absurd. If they are to be named at all they should be given permanent names for everyone's benefit. In the second place, however, the idea that this would benefit tourists is fantastically naive. The traveler cannot walk around Tokyo. The fact that streets have names will not make it any easier for him to ride streetcars, buses, etc., to where he wants to go. He cannot jump into a taxicab and say: "1347 Samurai Street, please". The driver not only would not understand him but would never have heard of "Samurai Street" and if he had, an arbitrarily picked street number would mean absolutely nothing to him. Finally, if he should happen to understand fully what the would-be passenger said he would probably die laughing.

To help the traveler overcome this very real and very frustrating obstacle, I recently developed and put on the market a self-guide system, called the DE MENTE TAXI-GUIDE TO TOKYO, which makes it possible for the traveler—or the Japanese, as far as that is concerned—to come and go in Tokyo with a great deal more ease and facility than has been possible in the past. (In fact, some of my first customers for the system, which is designed to fit a shirt-pocket or purse—were experienced Japanese guides who make their living leading travelers around Tokyo.)

The system is based on a device traditionally used by the Japanese themselves for their own private purposes. The first thing a Japanese does when he is to go some place he hasn't been before, or when someone is to visit his home, is to draw as detailed a map as possible. I took this idea, refined and systematized it and made it applicable to places the traveler generally visits, might like to visit or in some cases has to visit. This includes hotels, shops, travel and transportation offices, theaters, restaurants, nightclubs, doctors, dentists, hospitals, and a number of the most likely "tourist" attractions within taxi distance. The system is oriented primarily for taxi or limousine drivers but can be utilized in a number of other ways. It is available at the book stores of leading hotels in Tokyo and at various Japan Travel Bureau offices. Price is ¥300 in Japan and $1.00 in other countries.

XII   *Weather . . . for Better or Worse*

Official travel literature on Japan seldom does more than mention weather. Most books and brochures slide over this subject by saying that Japan has a temperate climate; and then giving mean temperatures for summer and winter. Rainfall in inches per year is sometimes added.

Being from Phoenix, Arizona, I find it hard to be objective about the weather in Japan, so I polled fifty foreign residents for their views on the subject and found that we all had one thing in common: nobody liked it.

On a yearly basis, I would say Japan has somewhere around thirty days of near perfect weather, when it is neither too hot nor too cold, the wind is not blowing too hard and skies are clear. These days invariably follow a heavy, fairly long rain or storm of some kind.

Then we have another thirty days or so in which one or more of the four factors named above are absent but the remaining ones are in a combination that still offers "good" weather. For example, it may be quite cold but clear and beautiful, or warm and windy but clear.

Other than these approximately sixty days of "good" weather, it ranges from some degree of irritating to awful. The best months are April-May and October-November. It may snow in April and typhoons often come as late as November, but on the average, these are the most pleasant months. Any other time the traveler should be prepared to put up with rain, cloudy days, or muggy heat from June thru September; or rain, cloudy days and/or blustery cold from December thru March.

A general rule-of-thumb for these off-seasons is one "good" day, three "fair" and three "poor" per week.

XIII *"Packing Them In"*

Japan is proud of its transportation system. The Japanese like to claim that their trains are more punctual than any other trains in the world. They are also said to be the only thing in Japan that is on time. Generally, both of these statements are true. You can set your watch by Japan's trains . . . . but very little else happens when expected so an accurate watch is of no special value.

Trains do, however, occasionally run late in Japan. Last year, for example, two thousand trains were delayed for what the Japan National Railway euphemistically terms "obstructions," but were actually people who hurled themselves into the paths of the trains as a means of committing suicide.

First-class on Japan's ordinary trains compares with second-class on American trains except that private compartments are available. What is now called first-class in Japan was called second-class up until 1960, and what is now second-class is the old third-class. The designations were changed but the accommodations remain the same.

Most foreign visitors to Japan travel on what is now first-class, and unless they are an extremely hardy breed and want to experience the "real Japan" come hell or high water, it is best that they continue doing so as there is a tremendous difference between first and second class. Not only are the accommodations in second-class much more spartan, there is no enforced limit to the number of passengers per coach and as a result they are usually packed, with people standing three and four deep in the aisles and very often in the spaces between the seats . . . . where those sitting ordinarily put their feet.

The result of this is that women lose shoes and purses, passengers suffer cracked ribs or dislocated shoulders; and occasionally babies strapped to their mothers' backs are smothered. When railway workers on a Yokohama-Tokyo commuter line called a strike a short while ago, so many passengers jammed into the few trains still running that windows cracked under the pressure.*

It is therefore very important for travelers to have their train reservations—(especially between Tokyo and the Kyoto-Nara area)—made as early as possible by local agencies, particularly if you are to be in Japan during the spring.

Trains running between Tokyo and Osaka—via Kyoto—carry several million passengers a year!

After trains, the most common type of transportation used by visiting travelers in Japan is the

---

* The day following this writing, it was announced that Tokyo's Chuo Line was then averaging one hundred broken windows per day from pressure caused by crowding.

bus. Where foreign tourists are concerned, the number of bus passengers is usually strictly controlled and everybody gets a seat. The biggest problem here is that the seats will invariably be just big enough to comfortably accommodate a ten-year old. The Japanese themselves find these tiny seats too small but they put up with them because of the traditional attitude that Japan is a small country of small people and all facilities should therefore be small—no matter what the inconvenience.

The sorry state of Japan's streets and roads, plus the over-crowding of vehicles and the many pedestrians, contributes to the discomfort of bus-riding. But this is a hardship that is generally bearable. The fact that bus manufacturers downgrade the importance of shock absorbers, however, is something else.

Very seriously, people with delicate constitutions are warned that it can be extremely painful and perhaps harmful to their health to take many of the long drawnout bus rides in and around tourist areas. Even a two-hour tour of Nara is enough to turn your liver over if you are not on guard. Much of the time it is necessary to hold on to the guard rail of the seat in front of you to help cushion the jolts. Most of the tourist attractions are outside of what is now Nara—old Nara was up in the foothills overlooking the present day city—and the roads to them are narrow, twisting and sieved with potholes.

Japan's best travel areas are on rail lines and bus riding can be kept down to where it is only a minor portion of the trip as far as distance is concerned. But buses are the usual mode of transportation once you leave the train station. The more affluent and those who are not traveling in groups often make use of limousines and standard sized "hire" cars which are available in most places in limited numbers. During the tourist season it is best to advise your travel agent if you prefer to utilize cars rather than buses.

Many visitors to Japan come here with the idea that they would like to rent a car and travel around the country on their own. It can be done but it is not advisable for any except the adventurous pioneer who has lots of time, patience and fortitude.

Except for a very few hundred miles, the roads and highways in Japan are like the poorest country and "county" roads in the U.S. Coupled with this, they are heavily traveled by vehicles of all types, particularly trucks that are notorious for their disregard for all safety rules and precautions.

Finally, it is difficult for someone who reads and speaks Japanese—including the Japanese—to go by car from place to place unless they have passed over the same road a number of times, because the maze of so-called highways and streets are either not clearly marked or not marked at all. For the first-time driver-tourist the problems presented by this situation are formidable indeed. These are further complicated by the lack of western style dining and rest room facilities along the way.

Not very many travelers to Japan have the occasion to utilize local city transportation, and this is fortunate. All facilities—trains, streetcars, subways and buses—are surely the most crowded in the world from about seven thirty to ten in the morning and from five to seven thirty in the evening. The old saying about packing them in like sardines doesn't do justice to the way people jam themselves into the cars in Japan's big cities.

During five years of daily commuting in Tokyo I seldom missed seeing at least one person a day injured from the pressure of countless bodies pushing them up against a wall or door.

It is so bad that most stations hire extra personnel during rush hours to help the platform attendants pack more people into the cars by pushing against those that are still hanging part-way out. Cars made to accommodate seventy people generally carry from three to four hundred.

Because constant closeness has long been a primary feature of Japanese life, they have developed habits that allow them to put up with such situations. In this case most of the standing passengers close their eyes, relax, and doze—depending upon the mass around them to hold them up. Everytime the train changes speed the whole mass sways backward or forward like a herd of cows. This is extremely dangerous, because very often there is enough "give" left to allow the mass of people to sway far enough to lose their balance and fall like a bunch of bowling pins, with thrashing feet and clawing hands playing havoc with your shoes and clothing.

Hundreds of times I have ridden from Shibuya Station to downtown Tokyo with only one foot on the floor and my body wedged into a lump of people at a forty-five degree angle, completely unable to straighten up or regain my balance. I was literally entombed in a mass of flesh and helpless until the train arrived at Shimbashi where several hundred people got off every morning. As many others will testify, this is not a pleasant experience and should be avoided if at all possible.

If a visitor should find it necessary to use local city trains, particularly during rush hours, it is best to try to board either first or last. If you are able to be one of the first aboard at your stop it is safest to station yourself in the corner formed by the door and the seat, turn your back to the crowd and not budge no matter how much buffeting this entails—of course, you have to know which doors are to open where you want to get off. If you pick the wrong side you may not make it.

If it happens that you get on last this means you have to step out of the car each time the doors open on your side, but this is a lot less dangerous than being in the middle of the crowd.

Above all, it is important to have a local service make your planned travel arrangements in advance when visiting Japan. Of all the problems travelers run into in Japan, none are so frustrating for the foreigner as trying to make his own train arrangements on short notice.

Over-crowding of transportation in Japan is not restricted to land facilities. The many boats and ferries used on lakes and in between islands more often than not are jammed with from two to eight times the number of passengers they are supposed to carry—and this brings on frequent disasters. Only recently a boat approved for a maximum of twenty persons started out across Kamae Bay with *two hundred and eighty* persons aboard. The ship sank just a few minutes after casting off its mooring lines, and several people drowned.

Travelers scheduled to take sightseeing cruises aboard small vessels on lakes and to offshore islands should beware of the possibility that the boat may become dangerously over-crowded with holidayers without notice. If it does, there is usually no choice but to get off; which is disappointing no doubt but better than courting death.

XIV The Traveler:
His Stomach and Manners

For years I have made it a practice to eavesdrop on foreign visitors in Japan to find out what pleased them and what had the opposite effect. It isn't necessary, however, to get closer than fifty yards to overhear the comments of a big percentage, especially when they are voicing their displeasure.

I happened to be standing outside a small restaurant in Kamakura last spring and was practically lifted off my feet by the voice of an American lady complaining about the service in the restaurant.

In a small grill in Osaka that caters to local foreign residents, I once heard an elderly American traveler rail at his Japanese guide for twenty minutes because the steak he ordered didn't look like or taste like "a steak should."

These two incidents are not by any means unusual. Rather they are so common that most Japanese concerned are used to such outbursts and look upon them as one of the things they have to put up with as long as they choose to cater to foreigners.

This common reaction by the American traveler

in Japan is a type of provincial, head-in-the-sand-stupidity that one might expect to find in a backwoods country hick but not in the class of people that has the imagination and means to visit the Orient.

If such people would stop to think before they begin making spectacles of themselves, they would realize that a Japanese cook anywhere except in a "tourist" or foreign restaurant should not be expected to know how to prepare American dishes the way they are in the U.S.

Some tourists rationalize and proclaim indignantly, "Well, if they want travelers to come here so badly, why don't they learn how to cook food that travelers can eat?" Perhaps they should, but this is like saying everybody should do what is right—a lament that is naive at best.

In each of Japan's six major cities there are many restaurants, usually catering to foreign residents and travelers, where excellent American food is served. In addition, there are a number of specialty resturants serving sea foods, sukiyaki and other "native" dishes (German, Italian, Hungarian, Korean, Chinese, etc.) that please most American palates.

Restaurants and grills in "name" western-style hotels in the larger cities are also generally good; although they may not be able to turn out meals that taste like the traveler's mother used to make.

Western style dishes in the hundreds of other restaurants, "snack bars" and "hash houses" that abound in every Japanese city may be very good—for the price—or very bad. A more accurate descriptive term for the food served in these places would probably be "Westernized Japanese food", since it is a kind of combination, and neither one nor the other.

Many old-time foreign residents in Japan, myself included, have developed a taste for its distinctive characteristics but the uninitiated traveler generally finds it much less appetizing.

As it happens, most native Japanese foods are not appreciated by the average foreigner. They are usually characterized by a harsh or flat taste. There are a number, however, like yaki-tori (grilled chicken) tempura (deep fat fried sea food and vegetables) whose taste is pleasing to most palates and are a treat travelers shouldn't miss.

Having accompanied more than one group of finicky eaters around Japan, I have discovered it is wise to take along little emergency kits of non-perishable foods if you are going off the traveler's beaten track. An empty or dissatisfied stomach will take much of the glow out of almost any tourist sight.

Service-wise, Japanese restaurants range from superb to impossible. In restaurants specializing in satisfying foreign clientele where the language problem is minimized, the service is usually as good as can be expected. But especially in the case of "typical" non-tourist Japanese restaurants where the help almost always does not speak or understand English—and the diner is just as handicapped—you never know what is going to happen.

Even when communication is no problem there is no certainty you will get what you want, as was brought out recently by Tokyo writer Kyoko Baba in her column, *None of My Business*. Under the headline "Poor service with a Smile", she wrote:

Japanese restaurant waitresses have the sweetest smile but offer the poorest service in the world.

Perhaps, they are so self-conscious about "how to smile sweetly" that they can't pay attention to what their customers are ordering. Often, they serve what they THINK the customer has ordered for they either don't care or don't want to ask back.

They can get away doing this with Japanese people who dislike to make scenes in public—an attitude which spoils the girls even more. But they can't do this when dealing with foreigners—like in this case:

"I ordered French toast, and not plain toast like this," said the weary foreigner.

"I'm sorry," answered the waitress, "but, we don't have French toast."

"It was on the menu, and that's why I ordered it. And when I ordered it, you nodded and went to the kitchen!"

"Just a minute." (She disappeared into the kitchen, then came back to the table.)

"French toast wasn't on the menu.

"Yes, it WAS on the menu. I saw it with my own eyes. Bring the menu, will you?"

"Just a minute." (She again walked away and came back to the table—but without the menu.)

"Our cook said he will SPECIALLY make the FRENCH toast for you but it will take a while."

"SPECIALLY? My Gawd! Why do you need to cook specially what is on the menu? Bring the menu, anyway!"

Again the waitress walked off, and finally brought the menu. The American customer gently held up his pencil, pointed it at her and said:

"Now, take this pencil and strike out the word 'FRENCH' from the words 'French Toast' on the menu."

Fact is, he had earlier ordered the okonomi-sando (mixed sandwiches) which he saw in the restaurant's show window. The amiable waitress had brought him a sandwich plate which was different from (and more expensive than) what he saw in the show window. But, to his protest, the waitress had stubbornly (yet with a charming smile) insisted that it was exactly what he ordered. He was annoyed but had given in.

Graciously, the same waitress had then brought him his second order—as a piece of plain toast. Well, she couldn't help finally admitting that French Toast was on the menu. This should have ended it. But, not in Japan! She served the "special" French toast without syrup. At the customer's cry for syrup, she disappeared again, only to return from the kitchen several times—but always coming back to the table empty handed.

Finally, she confessed to the customer that they didn't know what kind of syrup should be served with FRENCH toast, since

THE TOURIST AND THE REAL JAPAN 71

it was the first time they served that type
of food.

So, the customer had to eat the
FRENCH toast with the syrup for making
Pineapple Juice!

SUMMING UP: Travelers don't have to worry
about starving to death in Japan. They may experience many new and thoroughly satisfying foods if
they will put aside unnecessary prejudices and be
patient—but they should not come here expecting the
food or service to be "just like home" everywhere
they go.

XV *Prices High and Low*

Since the average traveler who comes to Japan must budget his resources, a few remarks on local prices should be of use. . . especially since most travelers in this category are generally surprised at the cost of the various "tourist" lines. United Press International recently carried a story entitled "Land of Rising Prices" which describes one aspect of the situation. To wit:

Does your shopping list look something like this?:

1. White pearl necklace (cultured) $15.00.
2. Black pearl necklace (choker okay) $12.50.
3. Kimono for wife, brother, $10.00 each.
4. Jade figurines (or earrings) about $15.00.
5. Japanese dolls $4.00 to $5.00 each.
6. Camera $25.00 to $50.00.

If so, tear the list up (in little pieces), cancel your trip and stay at home. This way your preconceived vision of Japan and shopping in Japan will stay intact.

Several hundred thousand visitors will holiday in Japan this year, and if they're like last year's, half of them will produce shopping lists like the one above and ask for help in their purchases. For some inexplicable reason, tourists landing in Japan think they're the first foreigners to set foot on Japanese soil since Townsend Harris came ashore on Saturday, August 23, 1856, as the first U.S. Consul and Minister to Japan.

They expect the natives to be out (in native costumes) stringing pearls on the beaches and giving them away for a few greenbacks or cigarettes.

Let's look at the facts for just a minute. Then you can withdraw another $1,000 or so from the bank before heading to the land of rising prices. The trip is worth the extra thousand anyway.

A good single strand of pearls will cost you $100 to $150 and up. Nothing less than $200 would do for a double strand of white pearls, this includes tax.

You can buy a beautiful pearl ring about the size of a mothball for $2,870.00. There are smaller and cheaper ones, and some even more expensive.

Of course you can buy the ones on your list for about $10 to $25, but you can get the same ones at home in ten cent stores. The

Japanese have been selling pearls for a long time and they know their value.

The true Japanese *Kimono* (with *haori* and *obi*) costs at least $100. Well-to-do Japanese families spend as much as $200 to $300 for a, *Kimono*. Wedding kimonos run up to $1,000 and $1,500. The father-of-the-bride pays through the nose just as his American counterpart does.

There are *Kimono* on the tourist rack for $15.00 and up, but you get what you pay for in Tokyo, too.

Jade is jade whether purchased in Tokyo or Hong Kong. No one buys a real jade figurine for less than $100 if you want to see it without a magnifying glass. If you're in the market for a family treasure piece, you can find it but it will cost you. The same goes for ivory.

Dolls run from $15.00 and on up. For less than this it won't make the journey home with you in the same condition you bought it. Japanese dolls sell for $100 to $150 in Tokyo department stores. And they're worth it!

Silk is a good buy and so is brocade, but it's not cheap. The hand-woven silk sells for $100 for about 30 yards. This is material for a kimono. The silk you will buy costs $1.75 and up a yard. Having it made to order for a dress or blouse is extra, but not expensive.

Cameras run about the same as they do

in the rest of the world, only there's larger variety and you save money by not having to pay the tax. Cameras run from as low as $10.00 to $375. A tourist can buy the best Japanese camera for about $375. With your shopping list now revised, you can plan on taking the wife nightclubbing in Tokyo (to keep her away from the shops). Drinking is expensive too. A night-out-on-the-town usually costs a party of four about $100. This gives you a good dinner and entrance to one or two of the better nightclubs.

If you don't bring your wife, however, you can take your hostess home with you. She is always feminine, and considerate, and usually asks for nothing. But you leave her a tip of about $15.00.

This vision of the Japanese woman always remains intact, before and after a visit to Japan. But everything else is very expensive, contrary to whatever you've been told or read. But it's still worth the trip.

SUMMING UP: The picture presented by UPI is certainly true, but it is not all the story. The price of pearls, for example, often depends almost as much on the shop where you buy them as on the little baubles themselves.

Japan Gray Line, a local tourist service, offers a four hour night on Tokyo for only $11 per person that includes a meal worthy of a gourmet, a visit to two name cabarets and one other attraction. This tour is regularly taken—and enjoyed—by top American movie stars, titled Englishmen, presidents and other top executives of some of the West's largest corporations. What's good enough for this sort of crowd should satisfy most of the less luminous.

As it happens, travelers who insist upon staying at the most expensive places, shopping at the most prestigeous shops and "putting on the dog" at the highest priced clubs would probably be insulted if offered anything less.

And it shouldn't be necessary to remind anyone that when he shops, eats or drinks in prestige places he will pay prestige prices. Surprising to many first-time visitors, Japan has more than its share of snob shops, bars, etc. In any of several dozen such places on the Ginza, for example, you can pay as much as five dollars for a glass of artificial orange juice. You can also go pub-crawling in the same area and have a ball for five dollars.

XVI *Is Bargaining Necessary?*

Many Americans who travel to Japan are under the impression that they are expected to bargain when making local purchases. They have read this somewhere or heard it from some would-be expert, or simply assume it because of a rather vague idea that all shopping outside the U.S.—and perhaps London and Paris—is a bazaar-like affair presided over by rascals whose sole purpose is to gip unwary travelers.

I have listened to obviously well-heeled travelers —usually women—harangue clerks in such prestigious places as Tokyo's Wako Department Store and Maruzen's Japan Craft Center because those hapless people would not bargain.

During the Occupation Days when so-called Ginza Street, downtown Tokyo's main shopping thoroughfare, was lined on both sides with hawkers' pushcart-stalls, bargaining was an accepted and common practice. These stalls disappeared from the Ginza's sidewalks in 1953 and bargaining went with them.

The misinformed or presumptious traveler who

tries to bargain in Japan today—unless he searches out blackmarket areas or sidewalk shops that still exist in certain places—is doing nobody a favor and contributes a little more to our overseas reputation as "ugly" Americans.

Hong Kong is a different matter. There are many shops catering to tourists there in which bargaining is usually necessary if you want to get a fair price. One shouldn't expect, however, to haggle over price at such places as Lane Crawford's.

All travelers visiting Japan naturally tend to patronize the same shops and stores . . . those that cater to tourists and are known to local residents as "tourist shops." Prices in these places also naturally tend to be higher than those prevailing in shops that cater to local trade.

Generally, however, this price differential is not unfair or unreasonable. First of all, these shops stock only items the traveler is most interested in, which helps save the traveler valuable time. Second, such shops are often authorized money changers and can also sell certain items tax free to the tourist. Third, recognized "tourist" shops are invariably staffed by clerks who speak enough English to communicate with the foreign shopper.

Fourth, by making themselves known through advertising and other means, such shops make it easier for travelers to locate sources of gifts and other "good buys" with the least amount of time and effort.

It is possible, of course, for travelers who have time and local contacts to go to wholsale districts and find excellent bargains. But there is no assurance that such people will find what they want and once they find it, that the price will have made the extra trouble worthwhile.

A good example of this was brought to my attention last week. A visitor staying at the Imperial wanted to buy a pearl necklace. He first went to a name pearl shop in the Imperial's basement arcade, but thought the prices were out of line. He found the name of another pearl dealer in a local newspaper, and wasted nearly half a day trying to find this second shop—not to mention taxi fare he had to pay.

This doesn't mean that the traveler should do his shopping in hotel arcades, which, in fact, are generally more expensive than outside shops—but it is foolish to go off half-cocked and waste several hours on the chance you might save only a small amount of money. Another consideration, brought out by one of the few expert and efficient travel counselors in Japan, is that most American tourists become shop-happy the moment they check into their hotel and immediately load up on everything they can afford.

"One of the pleasures of traveling is to be able to buy souvenirs or gifts in the areas where they are made. The traveler who buys all his Japan purchases in Tokyo not only forfeits this pleasure but pays from fifteen to fifty percent more than what he can get the same merchandise for outside of Tokyo," he said.

The best idea is to plan your shopping in advance, know the names and whereabouts of recommended stores in each area you are going to visit and consolidate your purchases when you have finished. It is therefore advisable to utilize the services of a travel agency that has a Tokyo office and is qualified—and willing—to advise you in this respect. A list of agencies which are most likely to be able to provide these services is included at the end of chapter 16. To save your guide money for more important occasions, I suggest you pick up a copy of the DE MENTE TAXI-GUIDE TO TOKYO for your Tokyo shopping. The guide is on sale at all leading hotels in Tokyo.

XVII *Good Guides and Bad*

Another problem that afflicts the Japan travel industry is that of guides. The situation as it exists was well-covered recently by a foreign columnist writing in a Tokyo newspaper. The occasion for his treatment of the subject was a story related to him by a lady friend who had lived in Tokyo for many years. He wrote:

She planned to take a trip to Gifu with some friends during the cormorant season. Time was limited, and the party only had two days and one night to spend in Gifu and Kyoto before returning to Tokyo.

Arangements were to be made through JTB. The lady painstakingly explained the tight time situation to a JTB man at the head office and asked him to book reservations, secure train tickets and hire a competent English-speaking guide.

"I had a few qualms," she said, "when I spoke to the JTB man. He couldn't even tell me the time of day. I was a bit worried because I didn't want anything to go wrong. I even checked in the almanac to see whether there was a full moon out on the night we planned to see the cormorant fishing. A friend of mine who went last year said that if there was a full moon the night would be too bright and the fish wouldn't be attraced to the fires in the boats.

"Anyway we got to Gifu, met our guide at the station, and proceeded to a hotel. Then we asked the guide to find out when everything started. He asked the hotel clerk—it seems he didn't know himself—and the clerk told us there wasn't any cormorant fishing that night. There had been a storm a few days before and the river was still too rough for the boats to go out. Why didn't the guide know this? He had been in Gifu for a week before we came.

"And that wasn't the end of it," she continued. "We decided to go on to Kyoto the next day. The guide who had met us in Gifu couldn't accompany us; he said that another guide was to meet us at Kyoto Station, take us to our hotel, and arrange tickets for a special tour we were to take there.

"Well we got to Kyoto Station and waited outside where the trolley cars stop. That's where our guide was to meet us. He didn't show up and we waited half an hour. We got tired of waiting and decided to try to find the hotel by ourselves. When we got to the hotel we found our guide waiting in the

lobby. I knew he was our guide the minute
I saw him. He was the most lost-looking soul
in the whole lobby—and he could hardly
speak a word of English.

"Then I asked him about the arrangements for the special tour which we were to
take. He didn't know anything about it. I
was embarrassed. He went to investigate
somewhere. When he came back he said the
tour was leaving almost immediately. We
all rushed off. By the time we got there the
tour had left. Believe me, I'll do all my touring by myself from now on."

But what about the poor people who
don't live here and who have no possibility
of touring by themselves? Those who can't
ask "ikura desuka" or which train goes to
Osaka? Are they to be left to guides who
know nothing, care less and can't communicate with them? Many tourists have similarly unpleasant experiences. This is not just
an exceptional case.

One source close to JTB said that lone
tourists or those traveling in small groups of
three or four are largely ignored because certain travel organizations are interested in
making money fast, and that can only be
done by taking care of extra-large groups,
like traveling glee clubs or visiting chamber
of commerce officials.

But in all fairness it must be said that
most guides, JTB or otherwise, are not so
villainous, lackadaisical or incoherent as the

two that the foreign resident had the misfortune to encounter.

It must be pointed out that a number are even outstanding. Joseph Grace of Everett Travel Service, said that one of the Guide Association men hired by Everett's was so popular with an American couple he accompanied through Japan, that they sponsored him to the U.S. and helped put him through university.

But why are some guides so incompetent? Karl Kircher of the American Express Travel Section helped explain the situation. Every guide must belong to the Guide Association, he said. The Guide Association appears to be very well intentioned, and makes all its members pass a rather stiff examination before they can qualify as guides.

According to Kircher, the examination consists primarily of questions on Japanese history and geography. "But not enough stress," he said, "is being placed on English language speaking ability. It is not so essential to have a guide who knows every shrine in Kumamoto Prefecture," he continued, "especially if he's assigned to the Nikko route. What the Guide Association should do is assign their guides to specific routes and then brief them on these routes. A guide shouldn't have to have a Ph. D. in ancient history, but he should be able to communicate with non-Japanese speaking tourists in understandable English."

The most important problem, Kircher stated, is money. There is not much money in the guide business. A qualified guide, one who has taken the examination and joined the Guide Association, has no ground salary. There is no guarantee of steady earnings. If and when he is employed, his pay is not bad. He earns ¥1,600 a day out of which fifteen to twenty percent is returned to the Guide Association in membership fees. In addition he receives ¥900 from the client for meals and ¥220 for staying expenses if he should have to remain somewhere overnight.

Intelligent young people (the average age of a guide is 23), who can pass the examination and speak passable English, are snapped up by business firms where they are guaranteed a basic salary each month, and have some chance for advancement. Not many want to become guides. Therefore the scarcity. And with the coming of innumerable tourists this year, Grace mentioned that there were so many he wouldn't "even venture to hazard a guess at the number," it is vitally important to send out guides who can communicate with their clients and are slightly interested in the job. Incompetent people stick out like sore thumbs while those who do their job steadily and well are out of sight, out of mind as soon as the tourist leaves.

In addition to the inability to understand and speak adequate English which hinders a big majority of Japan's licensed tourist guides, most of them also labor under a number of other handicaps. Because they cannot communicate clearly with travelers and because they are not familiar with the psychology of foreigners, they are not able to establish sufficient rapport with the people they meet, and travelers become a great deal more sensitive to their shortcomings.

I once accompanied a group of American visitors around Japan to study and report on the quality of the service rendered by the various guides assigned to them in different parts of Japan. Besides the communication problem, which was actually not too serious in this case, what caused the most friction was the tendency of the guides to treat the visitors like a herd of school children to be dragged from place to place, without the intellectual stimulation necessary to retain their interest.

The best way to increase your chances of having a good guide—and an interesting traveling companion at the same time—is to utilize the services of one of the smaller independent agencies. These agencies have to be pretty good to survive. They pay their guides and therefore attract better qualified personnel. If their rates are higher their services are worth it.

XVIII   *On the Practice of Tipping*

Tipping is a form of extortion that is now practiced on the gullible public in most countries of the world. In Japan, where gift-giving in the form of money or food, etc., has been an important part of social relationships for centuries, the practice (as it is carried on in the United States) is still relatively rare, however.

The primary reason why the custom has not developed more rapidly in present-day Japan, although it is becoming more common day by day, is because in their peculiar way, the Japanese long ago established not only when gifts were appropriate, who could give them to whom and what was appropriate as a gift for each particular situation, but also how gifts were to be wrapped and how they were to be presented. And, if anyone deviated from this meticulous, stereotyped arrangement it was a serious breach of etiquette that could and often did result in death for the person failing to observe the rules.

In fact, the system of gift-giving was so complicated that a detailed manual explaining all the different considerations had to be maintained and studied assiduously in order to keep up with all the regulations. So complex was this part of Japanese life that important personages invariably had in their employ a man whose sole function was to know the rules of gift-giving so he could advise his master whenever occasion arose . . . and it arose often. The various rules governing the presentation of a certain kind of fish to a superior person on New Year's, for example, required several pages of explanation and description.

Such a system, which was impregnated into the Japanese by centuries of severe conditioning and harsh sanctions, cannot be obliterated in a few years and must inevitably influence any new system of gift-giving that is introduced from the outside. As a result, the Japanese in most cases do not give or expect tips in western-style restaurants and few if any Japanese ever use red-caps at railway stations or tip people at hotels or inns who help them with their luggage.

On the other hand, many restaurants and hotel proprietors, especially those that cater to foreigners or travelers, have come up with a system of automatically adding ten percent to each guest's bill and calling it a "service charge."

This extra ten percent added to the guest's bill is ostensibly to take the place of individual tipping, and therefore most people, at least most foreigners, assume that it is later divided up and given to the employees who performed the services. In actual practice, however, the proprietors of these places do not divide this extra money among their employees as a special gratuity over and above their regular wages and bonuses. It is just ten percent added to their prices.

There are a few occasions when giving someone a tip in Japan is appropriate and a kind thing to do. The traveler will undoubtedly be aware when he has received service or attention above and beyond what would be expected under the most ideal circumstances, and the question of when to tip and how much should be a matter of his own conscience. Travelers will find, however, that almost every Japanese with whom they come into contact—outside of Government officials and clerks in bureaucratic organizations—will invariably give them considerably more service than they are used to, and a decision as to when and what to tip is often difficult to make unless you want to go around tipping everybody.

Furthermore, since the average Japanese are not like porters on American trains, they very often will refuse to accept tips and will feel extremely insulted if a tip is forced on them. They are not adverse to receiving gifts, but not immediately upon doing a favor for someone and not openly and crudely. Of course, guides and others who deal exclusively with foreign tourists are usually the type who are most likely to have overcome their aversion to accepting gifts outright, so the traveler is not always able to take advantage of the inherent kindness that characterizes what may still be called the average Japanese.

In any event, the custom of tipping must eventually become unpleasant or downright criminal, and speaking as a more or less permanent resident of Japan I feel it would be a pity to see it become any more prevalent than it is now.

XIX *The Toilet—A "Convenient Place"*

Some people may not consider it in good taste to discuss toilets in public but the unwary traveler in Japan may wish he had taken a course in Japanese toiletry before he finishes his tour. In a land as distinctive as Japan it should not be surprising to find that not only toilets but attitudes about toilets are distinctive as well. A recent Japanese book on toilets became a bestseller.

My first experience with a typical Japanese toilet occurred in the fall of 1949. A friend and I were watching a hockey match being staged at the Memorial Hall in Ryogoku, Tokyo. During an intermission we decided to go to the *O'benjo,* or the "convenient place."

As is usual for most of the older public buildings, train stations, etc., in Japan, there was no door to the toilet and nothing to prevent passersby from looking in except their own disinterest. My friend and I walked in, still carrying on a conversation, and went directly to a line of urinals in front of the door without so much as a glance around.

We were about half way through and were really enjoying ourselves—we had been drinking beer—when a titter of feminine laughter behind us caused both of us to look back. There on a slightly raised dais against the opposite wall sat a dozen or so girls on as many commodes.

My friend, who was the sensitive type, was so flabbergasted that he automatically tried to live up to American etiquette, and in the process splattered me and stained a good pair of his own trousers. When this happened, our audience went into peals of embarrassed giggling which showed no signs of letting up as we made our less than dignified exit.

A couple of years ago, I was in the New Yorker night-club in Tokyo's Shimbashi district with an American friend and his wife. During the course of the evening my friend's wife said that she would like to visit the lady's room—if there was "such a place." In this case there was, and I directed a hostess to lead her to it; jokingly adding that if she needed help to yell.

Well, the poor girl, who was quite a bit above average size even for American women, got into trouble all right. As it turned out, the toilet was a squat affair inside a cubic-shaped stall that measured only about three feet each way. She was able to get down all right but she couldn't get up. Finally, after several minutes of awkward straining, she did the only thing possible. She opened the door, duck-waddled out into the hallway and then stood up.

On another occasion, several friends and I were drinking in a small bar in Oji on the northside of Tokyo. It was a cold January night and no time to be going into unheated, windy places, but one of my companions decided he had to go.

The toilet was only a few feet down a dimly lit hallway and behind a flimsy door. Over the door, inset into the wall, was a tiny blue bulb which also served to throw a little light into the toilet.

My friend, who was in something of a hurry, opened the door and kind of backed in so he would be in the proper position—the place was hardly big enough to turn around in—and then he must have squatted without further ado because less than five seconds later he let out a cry of shock and rage that surely disturbed the whole neighborhood.

He had forgotten that the pit beneath most Japanese style toilets is not very deep and in the wintertime when there is not too much odor, they are often not cleaned until it is absolutely necessary. Being cold, things harden quickly and a fairly solid mound gradually builds up. On top of this mound there is usually a portion that is not completely hardened if the place is busy.

In this instance, the mound had built up so high that it actually protruded a good eight inches above the level of the floor—so when my friend sat down, he impaled himself on a pyramid of *unko*.

Only a few days ago another friend who operates a shopping service for tourists in Tokyo related an incident that happened to one of her "charges" during a buying spree. This time a lady, a very dignified and well-to-do lady, was directed to a public facility that happened to be entirely empty when she went in. There was the usual row of urinals along one wall and a series of private stalls along the other.

As soon as the erstwhile traveler had disappeared into one of the booths, my friend announced that she would rejoin the other ladies and they would continue shopping in an adjacent store. My friend and her troupe went on their way and time passed. Eventually one of the ladies expressed concern as to why their companion was taking so long. Rather than take a chance on being hasty, however, they let another ten minutes go by.

By this time it was obvious that something was wrong so my friend went back to the toilet and inquired in a very loud voice if Mrs. So and So was all right. There was an immediate reaction. The good lady let out an anguished cry, "Oh, I can't come out, I can't" My friend very solicitously asked her if she was ill or something.

"I'm all right," the answer came back.

"Then why don't you come out?" my friend countered.

"Everytime I open the door there's a man out there," wailed the traveler. She was thereupon rescued from what to her was a ghastly predicament.

Most if not all postwar private buildings—office buildings, department stores, etc.—in Japan boast Western, or "Westernized" facilities. These "Westernized" facilities are the squat-type but they consist of white porcelain and flush.

Out in the country-side or in public buildings like train stations, let the uninitiated beware. Except in a few places where special preparations have been made for foreigners, the facilities are primitive to say the least in most areas outside of the major cities and recognized foreign tourist hotels.

This situation points up one of the distinctive national characteristics of the Japanese. In their own homes they keep things scrupuously clean and neat but when they leave their homes and enter the public domain this concern for cleanliness and order vanishes. Public places outside of a few shrines and such are more often than not dirty and littered with trash. Public toilets, especially, are often indescribably filthy.

A friend who came through Haneda, Japan's international airport, just a few weeks ago reported that he was literally sickened by what he found in one of the main facilities there. He said he looked into every one of over a dozen stalls and found all of them looking like someone had sloshed them with a large bucket of "night soil."

This happens because many Japanese cannot or do not want to break the habit of squatting and prefer to climb up on a commode with their feet, rather than sit on it. If it happens to be a wet day—and there are many wet days in Japan—the first person who does this leaves mud all over the ring. During fair or foul days, however, it isn't long before someone inadvertently smears the top of the bowl. And since the Japanese are not as repelled by human excrement as most Westerners, others continue using the bowl until eventually it looks like a "honey" bucket exploded.

This sort of situation would not be surprising if it existed only in the backwoods areas of Japan. When it occurs on the country's doorsteps, so to speak, it is shocking to say the least. I should add, however, that this is undoubtedly not a very common occurrence at

Haneda or it would have been made public before. In any event, the incident described above took place in that part of the building handling domestic flights, on the day the Crown Price returned from an overseas visit when there was an unusually large number of visitors at the airport.

Last summer several groups of tourist included a climb up Mt. Fuji on their itinerary. I went along with one such group—for the fourth time—as a guide. Even with precautionary measures taken at Station Five (you can ride this far in a bus) where there is an outhouse type of affair, we ran into trouble. At each of the rest stops along the way there is a so-called *Obenjo*. But no self-respecting pig would go near them. Fortunately, we were climbing at night so members of our party were able to sneak off into the dark. During the daytime one can do little more than turn his back.

Travelers are advised, under all circumstances, to take preventive measures prior to leaving their hotel, and if they expect to be out running around all day to inquire if suitable facilities will be available. Places that invariably have clean, sanitary facilities include Japanese-style restaurants and *ryokan*, Japanese style hotel-inns. One or the other of these is never very far away from the traveler in Japan.

Travelers should not be upset by the sight of Japanese men—and children of both sexes—"piddling," as columnist John Holland calls it, in the streets. This is an old habit that cannot be broken quickly, and despite the fact that there is now considerable pressure among the more Western-oriented against the practice, it still flourishes. In one day and evening of running around in Tokyo, an observant sight-seer could probably spot no less than a hundred or so street "piddlers."

In addition to being unsanitary, public urination can also be hazardous. Not too long ago, two friends and I were standing on the platform at Oji Station waiting for a local train to downtown Tokyo. I was facing the tracks so I could check the incoming trains, while my friends had their backs to the tracks. We were standing fairly close to the end of the platform so that several cars had to pass us before the train came to a halt.

When our train approached the station I automatically glanced in its direction, and just as I did a woman who was sitting in the first coach of the train stuck her bare-butted baby girl out an open window. As the train began pulling into the station the little girl let loose a stream that literally swept the platform from one end to the other. I saw it coming and saved myself, but my friends—who didn't understand my warning yell—got wet-down like so many fire-plugs.

One last bit of advice: carry your own paper whenever you expect to be gone from your hotel for more than a few hours. . .you may need it.

FLASH—Word has just been received that the Kyoto Municipal Government has introduced a specially designed mobile rest-room pulled by a jeep for the exclusive use of foreign tourists. The restroom-on-wheels is painted light green and cost so much (an estimated $2,000) that the city fathers are afraid to disclose the price for fear the citizens of Kyoto would complain.

The fact that Kyoto city officials recognize the lack of adequate restroom facilities is commendable, but the idea of a mobile toilet cruising around the streets looking for "customers" (or would "patrons" be more apt) tickles my funnybone. I can see dignified matrons flagging the portable privy down on a busy thoroughfare, tying up traffic, while they powder their noses. Or a whole crowd of bus-rattled tourists lined up waiting their turn. One thing sure, any light green trailer truck in Kyoto better not stop in one place too long.

XX *The Business of Pleasure*

Many foreign businessmen coming to Japan have frequent occasion to complain about the business acumen of their Japanese counterparts, especially when it comes to how products are merchandised in the U.S. today.

These complaints are well-founded. But, there is one kind of business in Japan at which the Japanese are truly masters and which, if engaged in moderately, makes the obstacles that accompany all other kinds of business dealings here at least tolerable—if, it should be added, one is able to look at it from a philosophical rather than practical viewpoint.

This business at which the Japanese have few equals is known as *mizu shobai,* which literally translated means "water business" and refers to people and places that deal in pleasure and entertainment. The connotation of this descriptive term is that the "gay" trade is light, sparkling, not solid; and—probably—if taken in too large quantities, can drown one.

The business of catering to the flesh and to the mind has a long and unique history in Japan. From

earliest times, pleasure—both mental and physical—
was closely wedded to the everyday routine of living.
And unlike European-Western peoples who have often
sought to divorce pleasure or relegate it to the back-
gound as something essentially evil, the Japanese cul-
tivated the entertainment trades as a legitimate part
of existence.

A number of factors contributed to the flowering
of the *mizu* trades in Japan. These were headed by
the general absence of religious disapproval. In fact,
Shinto and various sects of Buddhism incorporated
the idea of taking pleasure in worldly things. Plus
this the trauma-producing discipline under which the
Japanese have lived throughout their history made it
necessary for them to have some method of escaping
this pressure at intervals frequent enough to preserve
their sanity.

In addition to several yearly festivals and other
occasions at which pleasure through eating, drinking,
singing and sex were the primary means of celebrat-
ing, entertainment districts were an integral part of
each community. (One other good reason why the gay
quarters flourished without undue pressure from any
source, was the fact that the so-called social diseases
were unknown in Japan until brought here by Euro-
peans.)

In these entertainment districts, which attracted
the intellectual, the elite, the rake and the lowly work-
man alike, the arts of pleasure were nourished and
pursued with consuming fever. A special language
grew up to meet the needs and fancies of the *mizu*
trade people and their patrons, and a special ethics
was developed to justify their way of life. It has been

said, and with much justification, that these were a race apart from Japan's farmer-peasants and the lordly *Samurai*.

Japan's *mizu-shobai-nin* had their golden age from the late 1600's to the early 1800's, and during these decades of peace their influence permeated the culture of the nation. To them and the people who came under their spell during this period, "Japan was the greatest country in the world, Yedo (Tokyo) the greatest city, and a being could ask for no more than to be born a man in Yedo, eat bonito at New Years, view the cherry blossoms in spring, and visit the gay quarters at night."

The world of the *mizu-shobai* survives today in only slightly altered forms. The gay quarters are no longer legal so the lights are not as bright as they used to be, and the demands of modern living have cut down on the people's leisure and raised the cost of pastimes. Their special code of conduct has suffered too, but the "floating world" still plays an important role in life in Japan.

Business and politics are more often conducted in ryokans, spas, bars and cabarets than in offices or conference rooms. It is simply impossible to close many business deals in Japan without taking part in one or more eating, drinking and playing bouts.

Travelers who would like to observe the *mizu-shobai* world while they are in Osaka should have someone take them through the Sennichimae, Shinsaibashi, Ebisubashi and Hozenji Yokocho areas, avoiding the big cabarets until the last or next to the last stop. In Tokyo the equivalent areas are the Ginza,

Shimbashi, Asakusa and parts of Shinjuku and Shibuya.

It is in these areas and among the *mizu-shobai-nin* that Westerners find the Japan they can most readily understand and appreciate.

XXI *Mixed Bathing for Everybody*

Contrary to a number of recently published travel reports on Japan, mixed bathing has not disappeared from the local scene. It is the rule rather than the exception throughout much of rural Japan. At most spas and vacation spots and in most of Japan's thousands of ryokan inns it is a matter of choice. What the above writers may have been referring to was the fact that a few years ago a law was passed requiring operators of public bathhouses to segregate the sexes.

Immediately after this law went into effect, many bathhouse proprietors "divided" the large, common pools by stringing a rope across them, and it was a number of years before separate facilities could be constructed. Others arranged for separate entrances and dressing rooms but once the bathers had stripped, everybody went into the same room.

Sex-conscious Americans find the idea of mixed bathing shocking or delightful, depending on the individuals, the circumstances and quite often the figure....a two hundred pound mass of flabby, naked, flesh—male or female—not being the most attractive thing to display....or behold.

My first experience with mixed bathing occurred several years ago in the mountains of Saitama Prefecture about seventy miles north of Tokyo. One cold, February weekend a friend and I took off for what was intended to be a two-day hiking trip. By the time we reached the hot-springs inn where we were to spend the night, the temperature had dropped to considerably below freezing. Since there was no heat other than what was given off by a bucket-sized charcoal brazier in our room, a maid suggested we take a hot bath shortly after our arrival.

As soon as we had shucked our clothing—in exchange for Japanese winter robes—one of the maids led us to the entrance room of the bath, told us to leave our robes in large wicker baskets provided for that purpose and then go on into the pool. We could hear a chorus of feminine voices coming from the bath area and would have backed out except that the maid who had guided us was still standing there enjoying our embarrassment.

Finally, we screwed up our courage, dropped our robes and took the big step. I will not deny that at that age I was much less sophisticated, and to walk naked into a room full of similarly attired bathers of both sexes required a great deal of effort.

As it turned out, however, there was only one sex in the room....all female. There were three old women in their sixty's or seventy's and about fifteen teen and pre-teenaged girls in the relatively small bath. Fortunately, the Japanese are used to seeing people in a state of undress and unless the newcomer is a foreigner they pay very little attention. Foreigners anywhere in Japan under any circumstances are stared at by the Japanese as if they were strange creatures from some far away land—which they are —and since a naked foreigner is even more exotic, there is a certain amount of staring when one enters a public or mixed bath. But it is far less than what you would expect because the Japanese consider staring especially impolite where nudity is concerned.

Anyway, in the dense steam filling this particular bath, our entrance went off almost unnoticed and within seconds we had merged in with the crowd. For the next several minutes I still entertained misgivings that some untoward and embarrassing incident might arise but it didn't and we were soon completely at home. In fact the cold snap became worse and we spent most of the weekend in the bath or seated around a *kotatsu,* a blanket-covered sunken charcoal pit.

Japanese baths are usually several degrees hotter than what most foreigners are accustomed to and this often causes problems—especially when the "tubs" are very large and cannot be easily or quickly cooled. First-time users should also beware of entering a Japanese bath shortly after drinking alcoholic beverages.

Some time ago, several friends and I were having a two-day party at the Takadakan Inn in Akabane. By about two o'clock in the morning things had started to drag and one of the group decided he would take a bath. He hadn't been gone more than five minutes when we heard all kinds of commotion coming from the area of the bathhouse. We immediately went to investigate and after pushing our way through a ring of about twenty other guests who were watching whatever was going on, we found our friend lying face-up and spread-eagled on the floor of the dressing room. The owner of the inn was giving him rapid artificial respiration by pressing on his stomach.

Within a minute or two after entering the bath he had passed out from the combined effects of beer and heat, and had sunk to the bottom of the bath. He would have drowned if it had not been for the fact that the maids at the Takadakan made it a practice to find some excuse to come into the bath when a guest was using it. In this case, one of them had come in to see "Red" and found him out cold and in the process of drowning.

In "Red's" case, the effects of the near fatal bout with a Japanese bath were temporary, for the next morning I was awakened much too early by the anguished cries of the inn proprietor who wanted me to come and save his gold fish. "Red" and another uninhibited member of the party who hadn't been to bed yet were wading around in the owner's patio pond trying to catch some fish for breakfast.

Travelers who restrict themselves to foreign style hotels have no opportunity to try Japanese-style bathing and this is a pity. It is one of the few physical pleasures of Japanese-style living . . . and one of the several Japanese customs that should be made universal—by force if necessary.

There are two primary benefits to be gained from Japanese-style bathing. First, it allows and encourages one to scrub himself thoroughly and wash all the grime away—one can do this in a shower but not in a Western style bath. And second, it calls for the bather to luxuriate in the hot water for as long as he cares to, relaxing not only his body but also his mind; both of which are good medicine for many ailments. One can soak in a Western bathtub, of course, but the psychological cleansing effect is much greater if you are well-scrubbed and clean and are soaking in water that is still clean.

Specifically, frequent bathing, especially in mineral baths which abound in Japan, is a well-known and highly recommended therapy for such ailments as neuralgia, rheumatism and certain skin diseases. There is also the companionship and a natural, healthy intimacy that helps prevent neuroses of many kinds.

Americans are primed to think of the naked body as a sacred "gift" that mortal eyes are not worthy to behold, and at the same time they are powerfully and irrevocably impressed with the idea that a naked body is the epitome of lust and evil. We are taught to think of sex as a furtive subject and are conditioned to engage in it furtively.

Most American men, in fact, are more stimulated by the surreptitious sight of a woman's dress pulled slightly above normal position than they are by the sight of a stripteaser down to her last leaf. Mixed bathing, if engaged in from birth, prevents such neurotic attitudes. Taken up at any time in life it helps one gain a healthier perspective and emphasizes the fact that the body is neither evil nor sacred, that these are diseases of the mind.

There are other potential benefits to be gained

from mass mixed bathing—besides pricking the balloon of the big-tit cult that prevails in the U.S. today. It encourages people to be more concerned about their body weight, since the close-up sight of loose blubber and/or skin-over-bones is not particularly pleasing, and cannot be hidden or disguised when one is naked.

There are over seven hundred commonly known hotspring vacation and tourist spas in Japan where mixed bathing is the rule for all except foreign guests, and foreigners may do so if they wish. No traveler who has come this far should miss spending at least a day and a night at a hotspring spa and enjoying an *ofuro*.

XXII *Should You Stay on the Beaten Track?*

As mentioned earlier, many tourists in Japan who have spent ten days or so dashing about from one guided tour to the next, very often feel they haven't seen or experienced the "real Japan" when the time comes to leave. Some of them keep muttering, "We should have gotten off the beaten track. We should have tried to meet ordinary people"—as opposed to travel guides and the people who make a business of catering to tourists.

First of all, it is difficult for the average non-experienced traveler to do more than just glimpse the real Japan. A foreign observer of the local scene, John Robb, has contended that it is the "policy" of the people in Japan's tourist industry to forcefully prevent travelers from meeting with Japan in the raw.

Robb's criticisms, aimed primarily at the Japan Travel Bureau, reflect the opinions of many experienced travelers who have visited Japan, and are therefore worth repeating in full. In an article entitled *The Two Japans*, he wrote:

In all the uproar about the so-called "two Chinas policy," no one except the penetrating Mr. Fisher of Fodor's Guides has been paying much attention to the "two Japans policy." This is not a policy you will find much discussed at the Gaimusho [Japan's Foreign Office] (the striped-pants gentlemen in that part of the woods being pretty much devoted to one Japan), but at the ever-growing Japan Travel Bureau, it is the holy writ.

When Mr. Fisher remarked in an interview with Maggy Burrows (a Tokyo columnist) a week or so ago that the JTB seemed to discourage individual travel at the expense of package tours under its all-protective wing, he was making the understatement of the year.

The perfidy of the Japan Travel Bureau is no new subject to this column, but I make no apology for returning to it.

News reports say that over 210,000 foreign tourists are expected in Japan this year, and the vast bulk of them will be shipped to odd points throughout the country in JTB "tours" which have all the originality of a cattle drive.

The average tourist seems to be treated like a rather weak-minded version of the little girls and boys who seem to wind on in endless excursions through the Japanese countryside.

So far as this observer can discern, there hasn't been a new idea in Japanese tourism since the end of the war (when most "tourists" were here under one form of duress or another).

What is the latest example of pompous inefficiency to set me off on another anti-JTB rampage? It

started last week when I was mulling over the interview with Mr. Fisher and thinking to myself with
some degree of self-satisfaction: "It's about time
someone did something to get the tourist out of the
rigid box into which the JTB tries to stuff him . . . "

The same day, I had some friends who had just
arrived from the far corners of the earth drop in on
me. They were youngish, responsible, highly-intel-
ligent people who had traveled extensively and who
were by no means the prototype of the demanding
tourist.

They were in something of a rage.

This was their first visit to Japan, but they were
unfortunate in having only about a week here. With
such a short time at their disposal, they had thought
it would ease their way and save time if they went
straight to the JTB and tried to work out some trips
to suit their ideas.

Gentle reader, if you've been here for more than
a few weeks, you can guess the remainder of the
story.

They wanted to go to Kyoto, but they felt they
would like to stay in a Japanese inn for a few nights.
Could the JTB arrange this?

The answer, as relayed by a thoroughly reliable
witness was: "Foreigners cannot stay in Japanese
inns; they will not be accepted. The best we can do
is to try to book you into a special Japanese inn that
caters to foreigners."

"But why can't we stay in a genuine Japanese
inn?" my friends asked.

"Ah, there are so many difficulties; foreigners

don't understand our customs, no English is spoken, no Western food, the inns think it is too much trouble."

Frustrated in their desire to see something of the "genuine" Japan, my friends sighed and left themselves in the none-too-gentle hands of the JTB.

Now the moral of my story is not that Japanese inns should in some way be forced to accept guests whom they do not desire, or that elderly and crotchety foreign tourist should be forced to endure the very real discomforts of a genuine Japanese inn—but that the JTB should act like a genuine travel agency and not like an Oriental version of Intourist.

No doubt it is impossible for the pimply-faced students and the half-baked bureaucrats currently employed by the JTB to tell from looking at and listening to the potential customer what he wants. Obviously, they should be replaced by clerks who know something about the travel business.

Helping tourists see Japan is not a bureaucratic task which can be carried out according to Regulation 36, Subsection b, Clause 4, Paragraph 39a.

It is compounded in large part of psychological sensitivity and a genuine desire to help. I have long been convinced that the JTB has neither.

All this poppycock about the "language barrier" and "foreigners can't understand our customs" should be exploded for once and for all. What the hell do local tourist officials think many foreigners come to Japan for, if it is not to dispel their ignorance about this country?

Instead they are presented with miserable imitations of European hotels and are forcibly (I don't think the term is too strong) prevented from getting in contact with the country as it really exists.

No wonder most of them return home convinced that all the talk about Japanese "imitation" and lack of originality is correct.

My friends did not speak a word of Japanese and had not the slightest idea of Japanese customs—but they were not boors or idiots. A simple pamphlet laying down the very elementary rules of conduct in Japanese inns (soap yourself outside the bath; remove your shoes before entering the premises; eat your meals in your room, etc.) would have overcome every difficulty that could not have been beaten by sign language.

The JTB seems irrevocably dedicated to the "two Japans policy." Perhaps there should also be two JTB's—one for the casual tourist, and one for the visitor who really wishes to see Japan.

The Japan Travel Bureau's rebuttal to Mr. Robb's column, while naturally designed to exonerate their reputation, nevertheless brings up some interesting and very valid considerations.

Shigeo Kimura, General Manager of the Foreign Tourist Department of the JTB wrote in reply to the above:

> We read the Yomiuri regularly in this office, finding it both interesting and informative. Columnist John Robb's observations on our country are enjoyable, and sometimes ruefully enlightening.
>
> His November 14 piece on the shortcom-

ings of the Japan Travel Bureau made us
wince. Similar complaints have arisen before, and we recognize that some of his
points were well taken.

Contrary to what Mr Robb may think,
we constantly seek ways of providing broad-
er, more flexible services for the more than
200,000 tourists who visit these shores an-
nually.

No doubt Mr Robb's friends could have
adapted readily to the Japanese mode of life,
and would have found staying in a Japanese
inn a delightful experience. In the pamphlets published by JTB, the Japan Tourist
Association and the Federation of Japan
Tourist Hotels, they might easily have ob-
tained a few helpful tips on how to conduct
themselves in a *RYOKAN*, along with some
handy phrases in Japanese, useful for re-
questing services at an inn.

It may be that in striving to meet the
needs of the overwhelming majority of
travelers to Japan, we have been guilty of
neglecting the desires of a few. We shall try
to be more observant.

Yet time and again we have made the
awkward discovery that the person who may
have insisted on being shown "the true Japan," harbored in his mind an idealized port-
rait of our nation that was flattering, but not
completely accurate. Those color photo-
graphs of Japanese inns in the slick maga-
zines do full justice to their grace and

beauty. Naturally, we are gratified when a traveler arrives, eager to experience such beauty at firsthand.

Then the complications arise.

We know that the room that presented such a lovely view of the garden made no allowances for screens, but our guests did not know this. After a sleepless night swatting mosquitos, the irate visitor changes accommodations and begins a lengthy correspondence regarding the amount of his rebate.

We take pardonable pride in the spacious symmetry of a Japanese room, and its appeal is appreciated by many of our visitors. Unfortunately, many find that taking every meal seated on the floor is less appealing, and quickly develop a renewed appreciation for Western furniture ("there's no place to put anything down!")

As objects d'art, many hibachi truly are handsome. As heating units, we must confess they leave something to be desired. And our visitors prudently are loathe to permit gas or kerosene flames in the room in which they intend to sleep. Apparently, sales of long woolies in the Western world lag far below sales in Japan, and the traditional local custom of sheathing one's self in several layers of clothing meets with resistance.

There simply is no substitute for central heating. The guest who contracts a severe cold or whose wife falls ill while touring under JTB guidance is likely to form an even lower opinion of our services than has Mr Robb.

Again, who but a very few, youthful travelers from the Occident are prepared to adapt uncomplainingly to Japanese toilets, particularly when using these facilities involves long walks down unheated, if picturesque, corridors?

Mr Robb, like ourselves, may enjoy the traditional Japanese breakfast of bean-curd soup and would seldom vary it. Possibly his friends, also, would have appreciated its excellent qualities. But there are many who consider breakfast and bacon synonymous, and we are in business to please.

In the main, we succeed. It is a universal rule that the satisfied customer remains silent, having received only his just due, while the dissatisfied customer very properly will make himself heard. Despite this truism, an impressive amount of fan mail pours into this office from all over the world, as returned travelers compliment us upon our service and thank individual members of our staff for small favors.

Lest these superlatives turn our heads, we can always open another file—fortunately much smaller—in· which are listed complaints we have received. These are thoroughly investigated in order to make certain that errors do not repeat, that book-ings are confirmed, and that guests are met at the hour at which they have been assured they will be met.

Despite our best efforts, occasionally we fail. Even with 240 offices throughout the country, our tourist trade is expanding so rapidly that we are hard-pressed to keep pace.

Knowing as we do that ten pleased clients do not make up for a displeased one, we are continually on the lookout for suggestions on ways of improving our services.

Where possible, we try to provide clients who request it with a Japanese-style room. This will have the tatami floor, sliding doors, tokonoma and other features of a Japanese room, to which the hotel management wisely has added screens, airconditioning, central heating and a choice of two menus, on one of which all fish will be cooked. Such establishments also will have Western toilets.

Is this too much pampering? We don't think so. Our guests deserve the best. Their comfort and health are our responsibility while they are with us.

Admittedly, the number of this type of Japanese room is limited, but it is growing rapidly, with more hotels and inns combining the best of two worlds. As such accommodations become widespread, more visitors will be able to savor the attractions of "the true Japan," without its former hazards.

And as they have in the past the staff

of the Japan Travel Bureau will continue to do all in their power to contribute to foreign visitors' enjoyment of Japan. To this end, we welcome all suggestions—even acid lectures by Mr Robb.

Having once been employed by JTB in the Overseas Travel Department and having also traveled about Japan in the guiding hand of the Bureau, I feel particularly qualified to add my comments to the above.

When Mr Robb accuses JTB of being, for the most part, staffed by people who are not capable of statisfactorily handling foreign tourists, he is right. The pay and prestige involved attracts—except for very few exceptions—a very low caliber of people. In view of the so-called importance of the industry to Japan there is no excuse for this situation.

When Mr Robb accuses JTB of being bureaucratic and rigid he is right again. This, however, is true of all Japanese organizations, especially those that have some connection with the Government, and it is naive to expect the Bureau to treat tourists as individuals. I do not by any means condone the bureaucratic attitude and behavior so well exemplified by JTB, but I do appreciate the fact that it is more of a national characteristic than the failing of, say, the executives of a company.

On the other hand, many of the points brought out by Mr Kimura cannot be denied. They are reasonable and pertinent—as they should be, coming from a man who is both astute and erudite; and who also can be reasonable and progressive in his thinking when he steps outside his bureauratic role.

Unfortunately, however, he is not representative of the personnel who staff JTB's hundreds of offices and come into daily contact with foreign travelers.

Mr Kimura has a counterpart in most such organizations and major firms in Japan. It is the primary job of this group of people to act as the "face" for Japan and their associates . . . whose behavior and attitudes the average foreigner often finds alien and bewildering.

Mr Kimura presents JTB as a hard-working, understaffed organization that does its sincere best, and he suggests that this best is pretty good. It all depends on whose yardstick you are using to measure the Bureau's performance, and in what context this measurement is made.

As far as getting off the beaten track is concerned (and therefore out of the "clutches" of JTB) it can be both dangerous and rewarding, depending on how you do it. During their candid periods, experienced and sincere travel service personnel in Tokyo often laugh at American tourists. They point out that many Americans come to Tokyo, spend a week or so rubber-necking and shopping in the vicinity of their hotel and then go home . . . telling themselves they have seen Japan.

In contrast to this, they emphasize, many European travelers go from Haneda airport or Yokohama port directly to some train station and head out toward a mountain, a famous scenic spot or spa, skipping Tokyo altogether. "These people come to see Japan and they do just that," they say.

From experience gained by accompanying tourists around Japan, listening to their complaints over the last ten years and running into them at odd places throughout the islands, I do not think it is at all wise for most American tourists—who seem to be elderly couples—to stray off on their own.

It is an excellent suggestion, however, for them to engage a guide-interpreter-companion and have a few experiences that they can have no other place in the world—and probably never again—if they are willing to put up with the few physical inconveniences mentioned by Mr Kimura. There are literally thousands of teenage boys and girls who would give almost anything to accompany responsible travelers around Japan, and they would do as good a job looking after them as a professional guide . . . without the objectionable traits that often seem to be standard equipment for the professionals.

There are also a number of local independent travel agents, some of them foreign, that will gladly provide this type of service. Here again, such arrangements should be made long before the traveler arrives in Japan. One of the most important lessons that can be learned about dealing with the Japanese in any capacity is to plan things in detail in advance. Chances are, if you fail to specify some detail that you think is so common you would be silly to mention it, you'll feel silly twice. The Japanese cannot be expected to think of or do what you think is obvious because to them it may not be.

Another pitfall not quite so common but serious when encountered by the traveler in an out-of-the-way place, is the difficulty of converting foreign currency into yen or getting someone to accept traveler's checks.

Last year, a very prominent Australian businessman, on my advice, went to central Kyushu to check
out several prefectural manufacturers. After a stay
of a number of days at a local hotel he started to pay
his bill but found he was short of yen.

His offer to pay with traveler's checks was refused. He went to the local bank and they also refused, saying they were not authorized to handle traveler's checks. From this point the situation went from
bad to worse. No one at the hotel spoke English and,
of course, the businessman spoke no Japanese. He
finally decided he would just take off and send the
money to the hotel from Fukuoka. But when he started to gather up his bags, the hotel proprietor called
the police.

The police, after considerable effort, got the idea
and were sharp enough to put in a long distance tele-
phone call to the nearest Japan Travel Bureau office.
The JTB office rose to the occasion and guaranteed
the hotel that they would accept responsibility for
paying the businessman's debts. Altogether this
consumed several anxious and painful hours, however,
and the erstwhile traveler let me know about it when
he got back to Tokyo.

Even in Tokyo, visitors who have large denomination traveler's checks are often upset by the fact that
it usually takes up to thirty minutes for a bank to
cash one of them. Japan has very strict currency
controls, banks are cautious and red tape is volumni-
ous. Agents here recommend that travelers carry
only small denomination checks.

XXIII *Why Visit Japan?*

Despite the cultural idiosyncrasies that make Japanese and Americans so different in manners and attitudes, most Americans who have been to Japan—especially the men—are very strongly attracted by life among the Japanese.

This attraction, which may be generalized into two categories, the intellectual and the sexual, is felt in both categories although the influence of the latter is probably the strongest and certainly the most obvious.

There are two sides—and several facets—to the intellectual category. The most important side is the very strong feeling of superiority that American men have over Japanese men—and to a lesser degree, that American women have over Japanese women. The average American living or traveling in Japan considers Japanese men vastly inferior. The ordinary American, in fact, is able to feel that he is better than even wealthy or famous Japanese, regardless of their character or learning.

The other side of the intellectual category, which

attracts all foreigners in varying degrees, even the most stupid ones, is that which appeals both consciously and subconsciously to the aesthetic sense, and to their admiration—from a distance—of some of the more benign aspects of Japan's unique civilization. Things Japanese that, in their own context, are pleasing to foreigners include traditional wearing apparel, handicrafts, architecture, landscape gardening, the rigid formality of Japanese "etiquette" and others.

There is also a very strong sense of the exotic surrounding everything that is typical of Old Japan, and this added dash of the romantic and mysterious contributes to the aesthetic pleasure experienced by foreigners confronted with a traditional Japanese scene.

The sexual category pertains only to men. The typical American attitude toward sex is that before marriage it is both evil and dirty and after marriage it suddenly becomes sanctified, but not to the point where it can be talked about in public without being obscene. In Japan sex has never had the stigma of evil. On the contrary, it is considered an important part of living and not only plays a leading role in the native religion of the country but is also sanctioned as a pleasure.

There have always been, however, different sexual moralities for men and women in Japan. Generally, all men considered that they had a right to unconcealed promiscuity, the degree depending only upon what each individual could afford, whereas the women were divided into two classes: those who were known as public women—which included prostitutes and usually girls and women who worked in tea houses, inns and other public places; and the home girls, the *ojosan,* who were brought up under very strict conditions and were usually, of course, the daughters of the better-to-do.

In the case of the *ojosan,* however, throughout most of Japan's history she has engaged in love affairs whenever possible and was not subject to pangs of moral guilt or any criticism stemming from a belief that chastity in itself was a "holy" virtue. About the only difference between the public and "private" women of Japan, as far as their attitude toward sexual morality was concerned, was time, place and partner.

In Old Japan, especially lower class women which included a big majority, but women of rank as well, were pretty much at the mercy of the proud, haughty *samurai* who carried their male prerogative as far as their audacity and means would allow. Legal and illegal redlight districts—for all classes—flourished until 1957.

In Japan today the situation is pretty much the same, except that there are no legal, and thus fewer, prostitutes but there are more "public" girls, and the *ojosan* is more apt to be abroad at night than the less fortunate girl who works in some office or store.

Since most Japanese men are as promiscuous as their financial position will allow, it takes a large number of women partners to keep up with the demand. Most of these are provided by the *mizu shobai* or entertainment trades, made up of bars, nightclubs, cabarets, etc—which in Japan employ several hundred thousand girls and women.

In addition to the one-time liaisons between customers of these business establishments and the girl employees, there is also widespread promiscuity among couples in the business and social world who become acquaintances and then date. This includes, of course, married men, who as a matter of fact, are usually in a much better position financially to carry on outside affairs because they are older and in higher income brackets.

Most of the girls concerned are single but it is not unusual for married women to have full-time or occasional lovers—especially since a large precentage of Japanese husbands not only carry on extra-martial affairs but also spend as many nights away from home as they can afford. A very large number of Japanese wives see their husbands only occasionally.

There are thousands of small inn-hotels throughout Japan that exist by renting rooms—and bath if desired—to couples who use them for only an hour or so. Most of the famous resort areas like Atami and Ito depend to a great extent upon the weekend patronage of unmarried couples to keep them flourishing. These weekend trips are very common and are referred to by men at least, as weekend honeymoons—and the men who go on them regularly, with different girls as often as possible, refer to their partners as "weekend brides."

I have known a number of men who boasted that they had had a different "weekend bride" almost every weekend for a period of several years.

Not having a deeply entrenched sense of guilt about indulging in sex, the Japanese look at it in an entirely different light than the average American, although the idea that a girl who is not a virgin has endangered her chances of making a good marriage has been present in Japan since olden times. It seems, however, that this belief is not nearly strong enough to counterbalance the other attitudes toward sex— one of which, in several parts of Japan, has been the practice of "trial" marriages by couples who were attracted to each other. The boy and girl lived together, usually in the girl's home, for a few weeks or months to find out if they could get along. If they couldn't, and the girl wasn't pregnant, the boy returned home and started looking somewhere else.

It should not be surprising, therefore, that when the average American finds himself in a society that still condones—in practice if no longer in principle— sexual promiscuity, he is apt to take to it like duck to water. Some, in fact go overboard. They are not content with a more or less full-time mistress or the occasional "short-time." They work at it systematically and take great pride in their "conquests." Two upstanding Americans I know once engaged in a contest to see which one could run up the longest string of free conquests in the shortest period of time. The winner had managed sixty-four—in a few days under three months—when a serious case of strain called a halt to the race. The loser had marked up forty-seven.

Another foreigner, who came to Japan on a cultural exchange-student arrangement, spent his entire stay of one year here trying to make school girl virgins; and according to his own account, succeeded admirably.

In addition to the attraction provided by actual, almost unlimited sexual contact, there is a sensualness and sexuality which pervades Japanese culture and gives off a constant promise of sex. This promise is a powerful stimulant to the average foreigner and it is the appeal of this peculiar atmosphere that holds many outsiders to Japan, rather than actual pleasures of the flesh.

Of course, much of the attractiveness of this promise is supplied by the foreigner's imagination; but there are in truth a number of qualities or characteristics possessed by most Japanese women—besides their easier accessibility—that give them definite advantages over the Western girl and often makes this promise a reality. These include many of the qualities traditionally considered ideal in a woman.

Lafcadio Hearn, the original Japanophile—who later, after he had had time to see behind the Japanese mask, severely criticized Japan's strange society —said the foreigner was attracted to Japan because it was like living in an illusion of some future paradise.

He said this illusion of paradise was provided by the etiquette cult of the Japanese which on the surface presented a picture of perfect harmony. Plus the old ideals of Shintoism, which included instinctive unselfishness, a universal sense of moral beauty and a common desire to find joy in life by making happiness for others.

For every example of a "bad" or obnoxious habit or manner that the Japanese have, a good or pleasing characteristic can also be pointed to and it is obvious that the good side outweighs the bad. In ten years of living in Japan, I have had so many special kindnesses shown to me that at times it has actually been embarrassing. Foreign visitors to Japan invariably encounter a number of such experiences among the

Japanese that are genuine—and oftentimes startling —demonstrations of unselfish kindness.

My younger sister Rebecca, who visited Japan last spring as a tourist, went off on her own one day to find the office of a steamship company. Quite naturally she was unable to find the proper building and in fact was in the wrong section of town when a man who couldn't speak English noticed her plight and somehow managed to understand what she was looking for. He then flagged a taxi and not only took her to the proper place but paid the taxi fare.

The following day the same sister forgot a pair of contact lenses in a taxi. She realized they were missing as soon as the taxi pulled away and tried to catch the driver's attention. He didn't see her but a passerby did, and immediately went to her assistance. When he understood that she had left something in the cab, he told her to report it to the police box down the street. When they couldn't find anyone in the police box, the good Samaritan, who was a young college student, stopped another passerby and explained the situation to him. The second passerby hailed a cab and took her to the district police station—altogether spending nearly an hour to help an utter stranger that he couldn't talk to.

Such incidents, as the above implies, are exceedingly common and although the long-time foreign resident often takes them for granted, the newcomer is immensely impressed and is enthusiastic in his praise for the Japanese.

This very strong human element, which is characteristic of the Japanese when they are in their own environment and at peace with themselves and others, helps make living and working—or traveling —in Japan not only tolerable but a little more often than not, more satisfying than what it would be in some other place.

Of all the much-publicized travel areas in the world, Japan is probably the best. The country offers magnificent natural scenery ranging from evocatively beautiful pine-clad coast-lines to the Seto Inland Sea, which has been described as "A Sight Fit for the Eyes of Kings." For those who like them, there are the well-preserved vestiges from Japan's strange past: castles, palaces, shrines and temples, which were built hundreds of years ago and have never been surpassed. In addition, there are the handicrafts, the arts, the architecture and many other facets of one of the most peculiar cultures ever to develop. Most important of all, however, are the people.

Descendants of an isolated, feudalistic society in which a certain type of formalized manners and aesthetic pursuits became accepted as the highest virtues—and homogeneous to a remarkable degree— the Japanese provide such a contrast of behavior and attitudes that few people can meet or associate with them without being tremendously affected. When this association is social and informal and takes place within situations familiar to the Japanese, they impress outsiders to a degree that has to be experienced to be believed. Many businessmen who buy millions of dollars worth of merchandise out of Japan yearly have said—and sincerely meant it—that they do business with Japan primarily because they like the people so much, because they get such a kick out of their frequent visits to Japan. And these are people who for years have had to contend with an endless stream of problems stemming primarily from the negative side of the peculiar Japanese character. Many experienced world travelers arriving in Japan for the first time have been lavish in their praise for Japan as a travel area. They say that Europe cannot compare . . . and these are unsolicited testimonies which cannot be denied.

Japan affords the traveler an opportunity to experience life in a society that, as many astute foreigners have observed, is "out of this world"; strange and yet provocatively interesting. Perhaps one way of suggesting what faces the traveler to Japan—once he gets away from the Western innovations—would be to imagine a trip to an island kingdom that had been "lost" to the rest of the world for more than twenty centuries and developed many attitudes, manners and arts independent of the things that make up Western civilization. A kind of Atlantis, if you want to stretch your imagination a bit. This, if you throw in the unpleasant and ugly along with the pleasing and the beautiful, is Japan.

XXIV *Every Traveler's Problem*

Pentathlon champion George Lambert, who is also a social psychologist and an "old Japan hand," once described the mistakes made by people who suddenly find themselves in a strange country as a "comedy of cross-cultural errors." Many of the errors travelers make are, in fact, sources of harmless humor and the term comedy applies well enough. Others, however, are more in the nature of a tragedy.

To avoid the more serious errors, it behooves the prospective traveler to do a certain amount of research on Japan before beginning his journey; and, as the Japanese are so fond of saying, "self-reflect" on his own likes and dislikes. He may find, for example, that his ability to perceive and appreciate aesthetic quality is so little developed, or his interest in historical relics so minor, that much of a typical "tourist" tour would be boring. Again comparing Americans with European travelers, most travelers from Europe have studied Japan very thoroughly before they start their trip. Whereas, as an outspoken airlines representative said, most Americans who come to Japan have never read anything about the country other than PR handouts, and "could care less." Travelers who leave their itinerary up to agents naturally get the standard serving of ancient Japanalia, spiced up here and there with something a little more lively, of course, but nevertheless routine.

Japan is rich in both natural and man-made tourist attractions that are outstanding. The problem facing the traveler is which and how many of these should he attempt to take in. Generally, one Shinto shrine, one Buddhist temple, one castle and one palace are more than sufficient for all except the student of such artifacts. Once this is taken care of, the traveler has a choice of several particular attractions like the giant image of Buddha at Nara, the "hell springs" of Beppu, the "atom bomb cities", a pearl farm, perhaps a silk factory and others.

Again generally speaking, travelers find everyday modern scenes in Japan far more interesting and memorable than historical relics. For example, the world famous image of Buddha at Kamakura attracts tens of thousands of people every year. Yet if the viewer is not familiar with the history of Kamakura and cannot visualize the statue as a direct link with Japan's past, it becomes nothing more than a big chunk of metal sitting out in the open. Unless the traveler can in his own mind reconstruct Kamakura during its heyday with at least part of the trappings of the times, he may as well look at a postcard. In fact, he is better off looking at a nice colored postcard because Kamakura today is a quiet, singularly unimpressive, crowded town whose only genuine claim to fame is the number of famous writers who live there.

On the other hand, the traveler needs no special imaginative facilities or preparation to appreciate a great many things in modern-day Japanese life. All the color, excitement and exoticism the traveler usually associates with far away places can be had in abundance in just routine living in Japan.

All the traveler has to do is participate in what is going on in Japan daily to get more out of his trip than he bargained for. As mentioned in Chapter Four, the average visitor is far more impressed and pleased with a few hours "on the town" than he is with ten days of trooping around well-worn tourists paths.

I am not suggesting that travelers avoid all of the various historical monuments in Japan. Many are truly remarkable sights and well worth seeing, even for those whose appreciation is generally limited to the so-called vulgar aspects of Japan's culture. If, in addition to a choice few of the standard tourist attractions, the traveler will do only half or so of the following, his trip will be successful:

Stay at least one day and night in a Japanese ryokan* inn; eat tempura and sukiyaki at strictly Japanese restaurants; visit at least two of the more spectacular coffee shops, two cabarets, two jazz-coffee

---

* The traveler who decides to stay in a ryokan should keep in mind the points brought out by Mr Kimura (ch. 22) so as not to be surprised or disappointed. I must say, however, that I stayed in ryokan dozens of times shortly after arriving in Japan many years ago—before I became "acclimatized"—and except for getting slightly stiff from sleeping on the floor, the experiences were thoroughly enjoyable. One other point: The room charges at ryokan differ according to the size and "architectural superiority" of the room, and also "according to the quality of the furniture and whether or not the room has such

houses and two specialty bars (like the Albion or New
Yorker) ; watch one afternoon of sumo; take in a
couple of hours of kabuki; take a number of "slum-
ming" walks through the *mizu-shobai* entertainment
areas of Tokyo or Osaka or both; visit the home of
an ordinary Japanese family; spend an hour or so in
a major department store; have someone take you to
a neighborhood shopping area where housewives buy
their daily necessities; go to a small village, prefer-
ably one along the seacoast where they invariably
combine farming and fishing, and stay as long as possible.

Visit a hot spring spa on an overnight trip; use
the subway and local trains once or twice during slack
hours; meet as many people as you can outside of
hotel lobbies and in addition to travel agents; visit a
Japanese grade school (I believe any school in Japan
would give you the royal tour at any time and without
prior notice) ; take in two festivals if possible, one for
children and one of the large, elaborate ones; and finally, have someone outline the plots in advance and
see two or three Japanese movies . . . a *chambara*—
a samurai picture which is the equivalent of the
American western—a comedy and a drama.

Above all, don't tie yourself down with an impossible schedule in several cities just so you can say
you've been there. If you do, at the end of your trip

conveniences as bath, toilet and wash basin." Therefore, if
your room contains an unusually rare and beautiful piece of
bamboo or cypress as a part of the fixtures, you will pay for the
privilege of "living with it." Summing up: Something the
visitor shouldn't miss.

you'll find your vacation and money gone and your memories vague and jumbled. It would be best to do a few places, like Tokyo, Kyoto, and Nara if you have less than a week. Then add one place for every two days over this.

XXV *The "Secret" of Japan's Success*

In addition to the human element that cancels out many of the habits and attitudes of the Japanese which the average foreigner finds negative or incompatible, there are other factors, psychological and sociological, that explain why the Japanese, despite their many failings are a formidable race and why Japan is one of the world's top industrial powers.

The first and most important of these factors is the willingness of the Japanese to sacrifice. From earliest times the Japanese have been taught and conditioned to believe that it is a virtue to sacrifice their time, their labor and whenever necessary their life, to fulfill the various obligations that are the essence of their society.

This willingness to sacrifice has been the one prevailing philosophy by which the people have lived and which made possible the development of all the various habits and attitudes that distinguish the Japanese from other people. It is visible in every aspect of their culture.

On the heels of this willingness to sacrifice came

a willingness to be regimented and homogenized. The Japanese became alike mentally and socially to such an extent that they more or less functioned as a single unit; one giant family with a common head. The secret of the nation's rise to power in the modern world is simply that everybody worked together for the same end and for considerably less personal benefit than workers in other industrial countries. Japan maintains its position today because of the same reasons.

Another factor that also tempers to a great extent the harsher aspects of Japanese culture and at the same time contributes greatly to the industrial prowess of Japan, is the very deep and broad stream of aestheticism that flows in every Japanese.

In addition to being trained in aesthetics from childhood, the Japanese seem to inherit not only a sense of but a desire for harmony in all things; in their selection of colors, lines, dimensions, speech and actions, including at least until recently, such violent ones as suicide. This aesthetic training and experience over numerous centuries eventually became a major characteristic of Japanese culture, a culture in which the people viewed themselves and the world about them through the impractical eyes of an artist whose chief aim was not to create anything new but to perfect, to do better what others had done before.

Of course, not all Japanese were able to indulge in formal aesthetic training and experience but in such a tiny, isolated country even the most rustic peasant or mountain hermit gradually absorbed on a lesser scale the preferences and attitudes of the people in the cities. Today the lowest laborer has very definite opinions on styling, decoration and decor and although he may not be able to explain his preferences in aesthetic terms, his feeling for harmony—almost an instinct—is one of the strongest compulsions of his nature.

This, however, does not hold true when he is confronted with Western products or Western ideas because his aesthetic sense is not cosmopolitan; it is entirely Japanese and without considerable Western influence, becomes useless to him when he is outside of his native surroundings.

Factors that played leading roles in the development of an aesthetic civilization in Japan include the powerful influence of Shinto and Buddhism, the capsule size of the country, the remarkable homogeneity of the people, the all-powerful feudal government under which the Japanese lived for so many centuries and, long before this, some peculiar trait in the people that seems to always have been present.

Together, these factors, overlapping as they did, provided the talent, the inspiration and the mold for Japan's traditional arts, crafts and pastimes — and once they had been developed to the point of perfection, the same factors also tended to prevent any change down to the present time.

One of the most interesting of the factors that shaped the minds of the Japanese was the role played by religions, particularly *Zen* as manifested in the tea ceremony. To those with only a cursory knowledge of Japan and the Japanese, to ascribe to the well-known but little understood tea ceremony anything other than 'tea with some rules' would no doubt be surprising, but to declare that the tea ceremony was one of the main fountainheads for much that is now called "Japanese" must sound strange indeed. Nevertheless, it is so.

The tea ceremony as practiced by the Japanese was essentially a worship of the imperfect; its adherents found beauty and elegance in what was bizarre and ugly. Unlike most people whose conception of beauty is formed by observing gorgeous, flawless objects—or by ear—the tea ceremonists made a cult of finding even greater beauty in flaws, crudeness, simplicity and naturalness—and their influence was one of the greatest forces in determining the characteristic form and style of Japan's manufactures and mode of living.

The tea room, the most important accessory in the tea ceremony, was a different world, free from all vulgarity; free from the slightest distraction, so that one could surrender himself completely to the adoration of natural beauty. It is unfortunate that this ceremony has not been better explained by the Japanese or better understood in the West, for what most foreigners considered a foolish demonstration of another Japanese idiosyncrasy was in reality the first time—and perhaps the last time—that man had made into a cult the unselfish appreciation of simple, natural beauty.

As a result of this remarkable aesthetic sense of the Japanese, there is a subtle charm and in many instances an exquisite beauty in the basic form and decorative design of native Japanese products. It is this peculiar charm and beauty, called *shibui* in Japanese, that has captured the imagination of the American public and done so much toward gaining wider acceptance for Japanese export products—although most of the Japanese-made products now being imported into the United States are not at all representative of good Japanese design.

Traditional Japanese merchandise combines characteristics that reflect the country's unique culture, especially the people's attitude toward beauty. Their love for refined simplicity, for naturalness, for humanness, for the subtle and the restrained, is clearly evident. Every Japanese to varying degrees has an artist's approach to all the actions of life—especially the little ones, from arranging food on a tray according to its color, proportions and even taste, to writing a letter.

One of the persons with whom I have talked about Japanese styling and decorative design is Mrs Antonin Raymond, wife of the well-known designer and a designer in her own right, who spent over thirty-five years in Japan. Her first reaction to my questions on things Japanese was surprise, and then she very patiently explained that whether or not a person could see beauty in a Japanese product or appreciate its aesthetic qualities didn't depend so much upon the product as upon the person. She pointed out — as did several of my Japanese friends later—that people see beauty in different things and to different degrees, depending upon their own experience, education and nature.

In other remarks at random, Mrs Raymond warned of the pitfalls facing people interested in purchasing products that truly reflect the spirit of Japanese design. Synthetic materials are to be avoided, as are additions like wire on a bamboo basket—because it does not harmonize with the material. She agreed, of course, that wire used on bamboo baskets added to their strength and durability, but at the same time she pointed out that it spoiled their aesthetic quality. She added that her own explanation of things Japanese was that they have natural logic and function without much mechanism, pointing to a lacquered tin can—for storing crackers, cookies, tea—as an example.

"They have a stark simplicity and purposefulness. And the Japanese craftsmen have an inherent respect for the materials they use. They strive to make wood look like wood, lacquer like lacquer, and emphasize the aesthetic qualities of the material." Adding, "Much of the charm of Japanese handicrafts lies in their imperfections. They do not have a machine exactitude that must eventually become monotonous. And this close contact with materials enriches life and makes it so human in Japan."

These factors are Japan's sources of strength. They are no longer stable factors, however. They are crumbling at the base at what amounts to a rapid pace, and will become less and less important as time passes. It can only be hoped that new and adequate values will be developed as the old ones disappear.

SUMMING UP: On the basis of interviews and conversations with hundreds of foreign visitors to Japan plus comparing my own travel experiences in a dozen countries, Japan, despite the pitfalls, offers the Western tourist more than any other country.

The traveler who gets the most out of his trip is the one who comes as a student, or impartial observer; not as someone who is doing the Japanese a favor by his presence.

XXVI   *A Capsule History*

Man first appeared in Japan several thousand years before the birth of Christ—probably before the American Indians arrived in North America. These first people in Japan were Caucasian, big of stature, fair-skinned and very hairy. Called *Ainu* (also *Emishi,* and *Ezo-jin*), they populated all the islands. Then some ten thousand or more years ago, the ancestors of the present-day Japanese began to arrive in the islands. They did not all come from the same place or at the same time, but they were predominantly Mongoloid and most of them arrived from the Asian continent by way of the Korean Peninsula.

As the centuries passed these newcomers, who possessed a higher culture than the *Ainu,* pushed the Caucasian tribesmen farther and farther northward, and according to Japanese legends, enthroned their first Emperor in 660 B.C. in Yamato near present-day Osaka.

During these turbulent centuries—as during the following ones—the Japanese were divided into clans at whose head was a chieftain. Their religion was

Shinto, a worship of nature—everything in nature housed a divine spirit to be awarded some degree of reverence. The Japanese lived primarily by farming and fishing. Tribal government was religious in form with the result that chief and high priest were usually the same thing. All official acts were carried out with great ceremony; some solemn and beautiful and others barbaric and cruel.

About 200 A.D., the tribe that had settled in Yamato gained overall supremacy and firmly established itself as the Imperial clan — guaranteeing a dynasty that continues today. By this time, contact with the Asian continent was regular and many of the arts of China, like weaving, shipbuilding, smithery and tanning were introduced into the country. Buddhism and Confucianism were also brought in and assimilated. With this advent of Chinese influence, the character of Japanese life began to change. Cities grew up and government was to some extent based on traditional Chinese concepts. The Emperor was sacred and all-powerful. Court life and court ranks became extremely formalized, and dress, style and elegance became paramount in the lives of the nobility and ruling families. The peasant's life did not change. It remained simple and hard and often times unbelievably harsh.

By the early 600's the Soga clan had grown so powerful that Soga became the virtual ruler of the country and while he made and unmade emperors at will, he chose to continue the Imperial dynasty as titular leaders of the kingdom while he exercised real power. Then in 645, another clan, the Fujiwara, overthrew the Soga and further prefected the pattern they had started—a pattern that was to endure for over 1,200 years.

There was much bloodshed during Fujiwara's struggle for power and after he took over he attempted to impose the Chinese system of government on the Japanese. All land was confiscated and redistributed according to a scheme of land allotments, with governors appointed to rule areas known as provinces. Territorial nobles who lost their lands as a result of this measure were awarded court titles and big yearly pensions—marking the beginning of an evil that was to plague Japan until 1868.

In 710 A.D., the Japanese laid out their first permanent capital at Nara on a grand, modernistic scale that would put many cities of today to shame. Temples, palaces and shrines which have never been surpassed—and still stand—were built. Art, religion, feuds and corruption flourished in Nara for seventy-four years, then without explanation, the capital was moved a short distance away to Nagaoka. Again, ten years later, it was moved to Kyoto. It was to remain in Kyoto for one thousand one hundred and seventy-five years. Kyoto rapidly became one of the largest cities on earth and the splendor of its religious and court life rivalled that anywhere in the world. Over these interminable years, the Fujiwara reigned supreme, but rich living brought indolence and finally weakness. Religious sects multiplied and extended their land holdings, eventually becoming so strong and militant that they seriously periled the Empire.

As conditions in the capital worsened, local clans in the countryside became stronger and began to ignore the orders of the central government. Gradually they formed a warrior class that was to spell the doom of the Fujiwara and the beginning of feudalist government in Japan. Finally, in the late 1100's one of the off-shoots of the Fujiwara rose to power and after a series of battles set up a form of government that existed until some ninety years ago.

The leader of this victorious clan, Minamoto Yoritomo, established his headquarters in Kamakura—eighteen miles south of present-day Yokohama — to escape the weakening influence of Kyoto. While Yoritomo exercised absolute power, he also chose to preserve the emperor system, and had himself named *Shogun* (generalissimo), a military title first used around 784 in campaigns against the *Ainu.*

The Minamoto family did not, however, remain long in control of the Kamakura government. Yoritomo died in 1199 and was succeeded by his two sons in turn, but neither was able to handle the affairs of state and their mother's family, the Hojo, took over as regents. Well organized and strong, the Hojo regency gave Japan forceful government for the next one hundred years—it was during this time that the Japanese fought off two attempted invasions by the Mongols (in 1274 and 1281).

But, the Hojo were unpopular and there were many revolts against them—some lead by dissatisfied *daimyo* (territorial barons) and others inspired by Emperor Toba II who wanted to regain real power for the throne. Also, large armies of warrior-monks raided Kyoto and the surrounding areas at will, killing and pillaging. Added to this were several severe earthquakes and a famine that left the streets and roads choked with the dead and dying.

All these calamities, coupled with the insidious weakness of soft living—which finally permeated even that austere city—brought the downfall of the Kamakura regents and the country erupted into civil war. In 1333, forces loyal to Emperor Daigo II captured Kamakura and burned it.

As could be expected, Daigo attempted to go back into time when the Emperors actually ruled, ignoring the strong daimyo who had helped him revive the power of the throne. This proved a costly mistake, and for the next fifty years the country was torn by wars between great barons, ostensibly to decide the Imperial succession, but actually to gain control for themselves.

By 1392 the Ashikaga were fixed in their position as the ruling family—and their reign lasted one hundred and eighty-one years. The first few decades of the Ashikaga or *Muromachi* period, were marked by bloody revolts. These were followed by several generations of peace. Then a gradual breakup of society culminated in more wars and the end of the era. The years of peace during *Muromachi* were a golden age. Gigantic gold and silver pavilions were built for single holidays which sometimes lasted for weeks. Life was gay and elegant in Kyoto and government was neglected.

In the country, the feudal *daimyo* became completely independent. Hardpressed and starving peasant-farmers began to riot and by 1467 civil wars were raging. They lasted off and on for the next one hundred and forty years.

Ashikaga Shoguns continued to hold the title until 1597 but rule had long since passed out of their hands and they lived a life of impotent luxury. Because of this powerlessness, many *daimyo* carved out empires for themselves, but of the two hundred and sixty feudal houses that existed in 1476 and the many that rose during the age of wars, all but a dozen had been obliterated by 1600. This period ended with the supremacy of the Tokugawa family, the founder of the last great feudal house of Japan. When Tokugawa Ieyasu, head of the clan, became paramount in Japan, he set out to make Yedo (Tokyo) not only the military and administrative capital but also the economic and cultural center as well.

Yedo, when Ieyasu first arrived there in 1590, was a tiny fishing village. Its only imposing feature was a giant castle built there in 1457 by Ota Dokan to guard the northern Provinces against the *Ainu* (to-day's Imperial Palace). Ieyasu changed all this. He caused Osaka merchants to move to Yedo and forced *daimyo* to build a home there and live there part of each year. People rushed in by the thousands and in a remarkably short time the population exploded to half a million. Ieyasu and his descendants attempted to perpetuate the feudalistic form of government begun by Yoritomo in the 1190's—and they were successful for two hundred and sixty-five years.

Briefly, as the decades passed, Japan's whole feudal system crumbled. The *daimyo* and proud samurai warriors found themselves competing more and more with wealthy merchants and a growing middle class, and in the end the merchants and middle class won.

All this pageantry and pathos, involving millions of people and so many centuries, took place in a country not as big as the state of Montana. The laws and customs of the country were rigid and harsh—no other people ever lived so long in such a restricted area under such prescribed conditions! And while many would like to believe that it all ended automatically, with the restoration of Emperor Meiji in 1868, it is not so.

Just over ninety years ago Japan was officially and actually a land of lords, warriors, serfs and slaves, keyed to a fantastic degree to a mode of life and thought that was unique to say the least.

It is also well to remember that the so-called industrialization of Japan was not a natural process but was imposed from the top—by the government—and that it is not yet fifty percent complete. This unnatural means of introducing industrialization to the country—unique at the time—was also responsible in part for the peculiar rules of "the Japanese Way" being applied to the business world. Happening as it did in the space of a few short years instead of several decades there was no time for absorbing a whole new philosophy and little mention was made of its existence. Attention was focused almost entirely on the technical aspects of industrialization — which was spread thinly over a full-fledged feudalistic kingdom that literally had just stepped four hundred years out of the past.

It is important for the West to understand Japan for both trade and political reasons. As one of the world's best customers and at the same time one of the biggest sources of manufactured goods, the country is a prime prize in the "cold war" for friends.

Other TUT BOOKS available:

BACHELOR'S HAWAII *by Boye de Mente*

BACHELOR'S JAPAN *by Boye de Mente*

BACHELOR'S MEXICO *by Boye de Mente*

A BOOK OF NEW ENGLAND LEGENDS AND FOLK LORE *by Samuel Adams Drake*

THE BUDDHA TREE *by Fumio Niwa; translated by Kenneth Strong*

CALABASHES AND KINGS: An Introduction to Hawaii *by Stanley D. Porteus*

CHINA COLLECTING IN AMERICA *by Alice Morse Earle*

CHINESE COOKING MADE EASY *by Rosy Tseng*

CHOI OI!: The Lighter Side of Vietnam *by Tony Zidek*

CONFUCIUS SAY *by Leo Shaw*

THE COUNTERFEITER and Other Stories *by Yasushi Inoue; translated by Leon Picon*

CURIOUS PUNISHMENTS OF BYGONE DAYS *by Alice Morse Earle*

CUSTOMS AND FASHIONS IN OLD NEW ENGLAND *by Alice Morse Earle*

DINING IN SPAIN *by Gerrie Beene and Lourdes Miranda King*

EXOTICS AND RETROSPECTIVES *by Lafcadio Hearn*

FIRST YOU TAKE A LEEK: A Guide to Elegant Eating Spiced with Culinary Capers *by Maxine J. Saltonstall*

FIVE WOMEN WHO LOVED LOVE *by Saikaku Ihara; translated by William Theodore de Bary*

A FLOWER DOES NOT TALK: Zen Essays *by Abbot Zenkei Shibayama of the Nanzenji*

FOLK LEGENDS OF JAPAN *by Richard M. Dorson*

GLEANINGS IN BUDDHA-FIELDS: Studies of Hand and Soul in the Far East *by Lafcadio Hearn*

GOING NATIVE IN HAWAII: A Poor Man's Guide to Paradise *by Timothy Head*

HAIKU IN ENGLISH *by Harold G. Henderson*

HARP OF BURMA *by Michio Takeyama; translated by Howard Hibbett*

HAWAII: End of the Rainbow *by Kazuo Miyamoto*

THE HAWAIIAN GUIDE BOOK for Travelers *by Henry M. Whitney*

HAWAIIAN PHRASE BOOK

HISTORIC MANSIONS AND HIGHWAYS AROUND BOSTON *by Samuel Adams Drake*

HISTORICAL AND GEOGRAPHICAL DICTIONARY OF JAPAN *by E. Papinot*

A HISTORY OF JAPANESE LITERATURE *by W. G. Aston*

HOMEMADE ICE CREAM AND SHERBERT *by Sheila MacNiven Cameron*

HOW TO READ CHARACTER: A New Illustrated Handbook of Phrenology and Physiognomy, for Students and Examiners *by Samuel R. Wells*

INDIAN RIBALDRY *by Randor Guy*

IN GHOSTLY JAPAN *by Lafcadio Hearn*

JAPAN: An Attempt at Interpretation *by Lafcadio Hearn*

THE JAPANESE ABACUS *by Takashi Kojima*

THE JAPANESE ARE LIKE THAT *by Ichiro Kawasaki*

JAPANESE ETIQUETTE: An Introduction *by the World Fellowship Committee of the Tokyo Y.W.C.A.*

THE JAPANESE FAIRY BOOK *compiled by Yei Theodora Ozaki*

JAPANESE FOLK-PLAYS: The Ink-Smeared Lady and Other Kyogen *translated by Shio Sakanishi*

JAPANESE FOOD AND COOKING *by Stuart Griffin*

JAPANESE HOMES AND THIER SURROUNDINGS *by Edward S. Morse*

A JAPANESE MISCELLANY *by Lafcadio Hearn*

JAPANESE RECIPES *by Tatsuji Tada*

JAPANESE TALES OF MYSTERY & IMAGINATION *by Edogawa Rampo; translated by James B. Harris*

JAPANESE THINGS: Being Notes on Various Subjects Connected with Japan *by Basil Hall Chamberlain*

THE JOKE'S ON JUDO *by Donn Draeger and Ken Tremayne*

THE KABUKI HANDBOOK *by Aubrey S. Halford and Giovanna M. Halford*

KAPPA *by Ryūnosuke Akutagawa; translated by Geoffrey Bownas*

KOKORO: Hints and Echoes of Japanese Inner Life *by Lafcadio Hearn*

KOREAN FOLK TALES *by Im Bang and Yi Ryuk; translated by James S. Gale*

KOTTŌ: Being Japanese Curios, with Sundry Cobwebs *by Lafcadio Hearn*

KWAIDAN: Stories and Studies of Strange Things *by Lafcadio Hearn*

LET'S STUDY JAPANESE *by Jun Maeda*

THE LIFE OF BUDDHA *by A. Ferdinand Herold*

MODERN JAPANESE PRINTS: A Contemporary Selection *edited by Yuji Abe*

MORE ZILCH: The Marine Corps' Most Guarded Secret *by Roy Delgado*

NIHONGI: Chronicles of Japan from the Earliest Times to A.D. 697 *by W. G. Aston*

OLD LANDMARKS AND HISTORIC PERSONAGES OF BOSTON *by Samuel Adams Drake*

ORIENTAL FORTUNE TELLING *by Jimmei Shimano; translated by Togo Taguchi*

PHYSICAL FITNESS: A Practical Program *by Clark Hatch*

POO POO MAKE PRANT GLOW *by Harvey Ward*

PROFILES OF MODERN AMERICAN AUTHORS *by Bernard Dekle*

READ JAPANESE TODAY *by Len Walsh*

SELF DEFENSE SIMPLIFIED IN PICTURES *by Don Hepler*

SHADOWINGS *by Lafcadio Hearn*

A SHORT SYNOPSIS OF THE MOST ESSENTIAL POINTS IN HAWAIIAN GRAMMAR *by W. D. Alexander*

THE STORY BAG: A Collection of Korean Folk Tales *by Kim So-un; translated by Setsu Higashi*

SUMI-E: An Introduction to Ink Painting *by Nanae Momiyama*

SUN-DIALS AND ROSES OF YESTERDAY *by Alice Morse Earle*

THE TEN FOOT SQUARE HUT AND TALES OF THE HEIKE: Being Two Thirteenth-century Japanese classics, the "Hojoki" and selections from the "Heike Monogatari" *translated by A. L. Sadler*

THIS SCORCHING EARTH *by Donald Richie*

TIMES-SQUARE SAMURAI or the Improbable Japanese Occupation of New York *by Robert B. Johnson and Billie Niles Chadbourne*

TO LIVE IN JAPAN *by Mary Lee O'Neal and Virginia Woodruff*

THE TOURIST AND THE REAL JAPAN *by Boye de Mente*

TOURS OF OKINAWA: A Souvenir Guide to Places of Interest *compiled by Gasei Higa, Isamu Fuchaku, and Zenkichi Toyama*

TWO CENTURIES OF COSTUME IN AMERICA *by Alice Morse Earle*

TYPHOON! TYPHOON! An Illustrated Haiku Sequence *by Lucile M. Bogue*

UNBEATEN TRACKS IN JAPAN: An Account of Travels in the Interior Including Visits to the Aborigines of Yezo and the Shrine of Nikko *by Isabella L. Bird*

ZILCH! The Marine Corps' Most Guarded Secret *by Roy Delgado*

Please order from your bookstore or write directly to:

CHARLES E. TUTTLE CO., INC.
Suido 1-chome, 2–6, Bunkyo-ku, Tokyo 112

or:

CHARLES E. TUTTLE CO., INC.
Rutland, Vermont 05701 U.S.A.